D1074909

EVENT HISTORY ANALYSIS

Applied Social Research Methods Series
Volume 28

APPLIED SOCIAL RESEARCH
METHODS SERIES

Series Editors:
LEONARD BICKMAN, Peabody College, Vanderbilt University, Nashville
DEBRA J. ROG, Vanderbilt University, Washington, DC

EVENT HISTORY ANALYSIS

Kazuo Yamaguchi

Applied Social Research Methods Series
Volume 28

SAGE PUBLICATIONS
The International Professional Publishers
Newbury Park   London   New Delhi

For information address:

SAGE Publications, Inc.
2455 Teller Road
Newbury Park, California 91320

SAGE Publications Ltd.
6 Bonhill Street
London EC2A 4PU
United Kingdom

SAGE Publications India Pvt. Ltd.
M-32 Market
Greater Kailash I
New Delhi 110 048 India

Printed in the United States of America

Library of Congress Cataloging-in-Publication Data

Yamaguchi, Kazuo.
   Event history analysis/ Kazuo Yamaguchi.
     p.   cm.—(Applied social research methods series; v. 28)
   Includes bibliographical references.
   ISBN 0-8039-3323-1 (cloth). —ISBN 0-8039-3324-X (pbk.)
   1. Event history analysis. I. Title. II. Series.
H61.Y347 1991
301—dc20   91-22007
                                          CIP

FIRST PRINTING, 1991

Sage Production Editor: Susan McElroy

Contents

Acknowledgments

I have benefited greatly from the comments of James S. Coleman, Clifford C. Clogg, Linda R. Ferguson, and Debra J. Rog on drafts of this book. I also received valuable input when I was planning the manuscript from Dennis P. Hogan, Lynne G. Zucker, and graduate students in my event history analysis course at UCLA. During the writing of drafts, I was supported by an NSF grant (#SES 9008163) and a UCLA Academic Senate grant for my research based on event history analysis.

—KAZUO YAMAGUCHI

1

Introduction

Event history analysis is concerned with the patterns and correlates of the occurrences of events. Social scientists study various kinds of events. Demographers, for example, study individual life events such as deaths, births, migrations, marriages, and divorces. Sociologists and labor economists study events of labor force participation and career processes such as employment and unemployment, interfirm and intrafirm job separations, and promotions and demotions. Criminologists study such events as crimes, arrests, and recidivism, and epidemiological researchers of drug abuse study initiation, cessation, and relapse of drug use. The events of interest to social scientists include not only life events of individuals, but also events that occur for organizations. Thus researchers in organizational studies and industrial relations study events such as deaths of organizations, mergers, and strikes.

By definition, occurrence of an event assumes a preceding time interval that represents its nonoccurrence. More specifically, a certain time period or *duration* of nonoccurrence must exist in order for an occurrence to be recognized as an "event." Event history analysis is used to study duration data, which represent the nonoccurrence of a given event. Hence the term *analysis of duration data* is used to refer to a broad range of techniques, including most of the methods and models that are introduced in this book.

The specification of duration data, however, may not uniquely define an event. An event is defined by specifying a group of end points for duration intervals. The group, however, may not include all end points for the duration intervals. For example, in the analysis of job histories, we can collect duration data on (a) the amount of time that an employee continuously held a particular job in the same firm, (b) the period of employment with the same employer irrespective of jobs held, or (c) the length of employment regardless of job type or employer. In the general case of employment, an event, such as becoming nonemployed, is defined by the end point of the duration interval for being employed. However, a distinct event can be defined for a specific subgroup of end points. That is, becoming nonemployed may refer either to becoming unemployed or to leaving the labor force (which may involve retirement, the decision to become a full-time homemaker, and so forth), which can be defined as distinct events. Similarly, interfirm job separation is an event that is defined by the end point of the duration interval for being employed by a particular employer. This event also includes distinct groups, such as (a) interfirm job change and (b) becoming nonemployed, which can be defined as distinct events. The end point of the duration interval for having a particular job in the same firm defines an event, job separation. The event also includes distinct groups, such as (a) intrafirm job change and (b) interfirm job separation, which can be defined as distinct events. Hence an event is defined by a specified group of end points for duration intervals.

In conceptualizing the duration of the nonoccurrence of a given event, another important concept is relevant: the *risk period*. Generally, we can divide the time period that represents the nonoccurrence of a given event into two parts: the period at risk and the period not at risk for having the event. For example, a divorce can occur to individuals only when they are married, and a job separation can occur to individuals only when they have a job. Individuals who are not married or who do not have jobs are not at risk for divorce or for having a job separation, respectively.

The distinction between the risk and nonrisk periods always requires an assumption. The assumption may be implicit, as in the case of divorce, for which we usually assume that individuals are at risk throughout the period of marriage. However, the risk period often requires a more explicit assumption. For example, we may not know exactly the beginning of the risk period for getting married. We may assume that all subjects enter the risk period at the same certain age, and may further equate this age with the youngest age of marriage observed in the particular sample of subjects. The particular assumption we make in defining the risk period becomes a characteristic of the model we employ in the analysis, and the adequacy of the assumption is crucial for making a good analysis. For a given definition of the risk period, we refer to a sample of persons who are at risk—that is, in their risk periods—for having the event at a given time as the *risk set* of that time.

Given the distinction between the risk and nonrisk periods, event history analysis can be defined either as the analysis of the *duration* for the nonoccurrence of an event *during the risk period* or as the analysis of *rates* of the occurrence of the event *during the risk period.*[1]

The rate usually varies with time and among groups. The rate, when attached to a particular moment in time, is often referred to as a *hazard rate* or *transition rate*. The term *hazard* comes from biostatistics, where the typical event is death. The term *transition rate* is more often used in sociology, where many analyses have been made of transitions between discrete states, such as occupational and employment statuses, based on the use of Markov and semi-Markov process models (e.g., Bartholomew, 1982; Coleman, 1964; Tuma, 1976). In this book, I use the term *hazard rates.*

There are two major groups of methods for analyzing hazard rates: *fully* or *partially parametric* (or *semiparametric*) methods and *non-parametric* methods. Fully or partially parametric methods estimate the effects of explanatory variables, called *covariates*, on hazard rates. For example, in the analysis of divorce, covariates that can be used include individual characteristics that do not vary throughout the duration of the marriage (such as race, educational attainment before marriage, and age at marriage) and time-varying individual characteristics (such as employment status and income). On the other hand, nonparametric methods do not specify the relation between hazard rates and explanatory variables. Instead, separate estimates of rates as a function of time are obtained for distinct "strata," such as ethnic groups, which are distinguished by a time-invariant categorical variable. Event history analysis usually refers to an analysis based on fully or partially parametric *hazard-rate models*. This book discusses methods based on these models exclusively.

CENSORING

One major advantage of hazard-rate models for the analysis of duration data, compared with some conventional methods such as linear regression analysis, is its capacity to deal with certain types of *censored observations*. *Censoring* exists when incomplete information is available about the duration of the risk period because of a limited observation period. Figure 1.1 depicts six distinct situations regarding

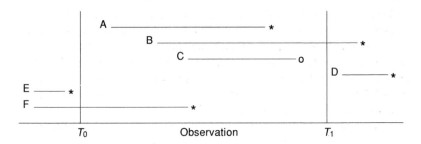

Figure 1.1. Right and Left Censored Observations
NOTE: * = occurrence of event of interest
o = occurrence of event other than event of interest

censored observations. Besides these six situations, some of their combinations are also possible. All subjects are under observation from time T_0 to time T_1 and we assume here that both T_0 and T_1 are determined independently of subjects. The solid line represents the risk period for each subject. The solid line with an asterisk (*) at the end point indicates an occurrence of the event of interest, and the solid line with an open end point (o) indicates that the risk period is terminated by an event other than the event of interest. For example, when the event of interest is an occurrence of involuntary job separation, the solid line, the end point *, and the end point o, respectively, indicate the period of employment, an occurrence of involuntary job separation, and an occurrence of voluntary job separation.

In order to understand differences in the type of censoring, it is useful to employ a typology of missing-data mechanisms introduced by Little and Rubin (1987, pp. 13-15). Using two variables X and Y, we can distinguish three distinct missing-data mechanisms. Variable Y is the dependent variable with nonresponse (i.e., missing data). In the present case, Y is the duration of the risk period up to the occurrence of the event, and is subject to nonresponse in the sample due to censoring. In the present case, variable X represents the timing of entry into the risk period. Generally, we can identify three distinct missing-data mechanisms according to whether the probability of nonresponse to Y (a) depends on Y (and possibly X as well), (b) depends on X but not on Y, or (c) is independent of X and Y.

Little and Rubin refer to case (c) as a situation in which the data are *missing completely at random* (MCAR), which occurs when the missing data are *missing at random* (MAR) and the observed data are *observed at random* (OAR). The data are not MAR when the non-response to Y depends on the value of Y, and the data are not OAR when the nonresponse to Y depends on the value of X. Therefore, if case (b) applies, the missing data are missing at random (i.e., MAR), but the observed data are not observed at random. In this case, the observed data are random only within levels of X. If case (a) applies, the data are neither MAR nor OAR.

If the missing data are not missing at random (i.e., not MAR), it is important to distinguish between situations where (a) the data of Y are missing by a *known mechanism* and (b) the data of Y are missing by an *unknown mechanism*. We have the most serious problem when the missing data are not MAR and are missing by an unknown mechanism.

We can apply this typology of missing-data mechanisms to the different types of censoring depicted in Figure 1.1. In Figure 1.1, the entire risk period for Subject A falls within the period of observation. There is no censoring for this observation.

The risk period of Subject B starts during the period of observation, and he or she has not had the event when the observation is terminated at time T_1. The subject's observation is *censored on the right* (or *right censored*) at T_1. This type of right censoring typically occurs at the survey date. Since we do not know the date of exit from the risk period for Subject B, the value of Y (i.e., the duration of the risk period up to the occurrence of the event) is missing even though we have information about the duration of the risk period up to the censoring time.

In order to make a distinction from the case of Subject D, discussed below, the case of Subject B is also called a *right-truncated* observation. Truncation is a special case of censoring that is characterized by a partial observation of the duration data. Given that the timing of T_1 is determined independently of the hazard rates, as in the case of censoring at a predetermined survey date,[2] event history analysis can handle this type of right censoring adequately. Among censored observations, right-truncated observations occur most frequently in social science studies, and the capacity of event history analysis to handle them is its major advantage over other analyses, such as linear or logit regression analyses in their conventional usage. In terms of Little and Rubin's typology, the missing data are not MAR but missing by a known mechanism for right-truncated observations. The missing data are not MAR because the occurrence of censoring depends on the value of Y; the mechanism is known because we know when and how the observations are right truncated.

The remaining four cases require additional explanations. For Subject C, the observation is right censored because an event other than the event of interest occurs during the observation period and takes the subject out of the risk set. This case will not be a problem if the event that terminated the observation occurred independently of the hazard rate of the event of interest. For example, in the analysis of marriage, the occurrence of death by an accident may be regarded as independent of the hazard rate of getting married. This is *independent* censoring. On the other hand, the occurrence of death due to disease may not be independent of the hazard rate of marriage because people have significantly reduced probabilities of marriage while they are ill. This type of censoring, called *nonindependent* censoring, is an issue in the analysis of competing events, which is discussed in Chapter 7. If censoring is independent of the event of interest, the case of Subject C can be treated as a right-censored observation technically in the same way as that for Subject B.

Subject D represents a case in which the observation is *fully censored on the right*. Entry into the risk period occurs after the observation period and, therefore, the value of Y is missing for Subject D. In other words, the occurrence of full right censoring depends only on the particular variable X that represents the timing of entry into the risk period and, therefore, does not depend on duration Y. Indeed, when $X < T_1$, we observe duration data (including right truncated case), and when $X \geq T_1$ we have no duration data (i.e., full right censoring). (Since we are concerned here only with right censoring, we assume $X \geq T_0$.) Hence, according to Little and Rubin's typology, the missing data of Y with fully right-censored cases are MAR, but the observed data of Y are not OAR. It follows that unless Y is statistically independent of X, the hazard rate model for duration variable Y has to take into account the effects of variable X on the hazard rate in order to eliminate the sample selection bias.

Let's take an example. Suppose we have a representative cross-sectional sample of a multiple-cohort population and collect data on marital histories at time T_1 for persons who are ever married. We intend to analyze the occurrence of divorce in the first marriage. Then, entry into the risk period (i.e., the value of variable X) is determined by the sum of year (and date) of birth and age (and date) of marriage. If the sum exceeds time T_1, we have full right censoring. It follows that the hazard rate model of divorce has to take into account both the effect of birth cohort and age of marriage in order to control for sample selection bias. In some cases, the values of X also specify a subpopulation for which the findings of the analysis can be generalized. For example, if we have data from a single cohort instead of multiple cohorts in the analysis of divorce described above, the value of X will correspond to a specific age of marriage. Then, the sample with responses in fact corresponds to a subpopulation of people with certain young ages of marriage.

In conclusion, the presence of Subject D leads to a situation in which the missing data are missing at random but the observed data are not observed at random. Therefore, the hazard rate model has to account for the possible effects of the timing of entry into the risk period on the hazard rate. In fact, if variable X has an effect on the hazard rate and the model does not take it into account, the model is misspecified regardless of the presence of fully right-censored cases. Hence the presence of fully right-censored observations only highlights a particular possible misspecification of the model.

The case of Subject E in Figure 1.1 represents a case with *full censoring on the left*. Generally, left censoring is much less manageable than right censoring, and the case of Subject E is the worst possible situation. Both entry into the risk period and exit from the risk period occur prior to the observation period, and, therefore, the value of Y is missing for subject E. The data with fully left-censored cases are neither MAR nor OAR. The observed data are not observed at random because the absence of duration data depends in part on the timing of entry into the risk period. The missing data are not missing at random because the absence of duration data depends on the duration of the risk period as well. In fact, all cases with full left censoring satisfy $X + Y < T_0$. Furthermore, the missing-data mechanism is *unknown* because we do not know when and how the event occurred to make the value of Y missing. Hence the sample selection bias generated by full left censoring is difficult to fix for two reasons. First, unlike the case of full right censoring, the sample selection bias occurs as a function of the unknown values of the dependent variable Y itself. Second, unlike the case of right truncation, the missing-data mechanism is unknown. Unless the number of subjects with full left censoring is negligibly small, there will be serious bias in parameter estimates.

The case of Subject F in Figure 1.1 represents a partially left-censored observation, which is also called *left truncation*. The problem here is different from the case of Subject E. A crucial question is whether we have data for X, the beginning of the risk period. If we do not, we cannot specify the initial value of duration at time T_0 for Subject F and, except for special cases that are discussed in Chapter 3, we cannot adequately use the data of Subject F. We cannot equate the beginning of the observation period with the beginning of the risk period for left-truncated duration data. Again, this is a situation where the missing data are not MAR and are missing by an unknown mechanism.

On the other hand, suppose we know the timing of entry into the risk period for Subject F and, therefore, the initial value of duration at time T_0. Then, *the value of Y is not missing.* However, we may not have data for *time-dependent covariates* (i.e., explanatory variables that vary over time) from the beginning of the risk period to the beginning of the observation period T_0. Then, given *full knowledge of the values of both duration and covariates during the period of observation*, we may adequately include in the analysis the data of *conditional* survival from time T_0 to the time the event occurred (or to the time of right censoring) for Subject F, given his or her survival at time T_0.[3]

It is worthwhile to note that if we omit *both* groups of left-truncated and fully left-censored observations from the analysis, the missing data are MAR but the observed data are not OAR. The probability of nonresponse then is independent of duration Y and depends only on the timing of entry into the risk period X. For example, we can analyze divorce among subjects who married at a prespecified time T_0 or later. Then, sample selection bias can be handled by taking into account the effect of the timing of entry into the risk set on the hazard rate. It is assumed here, however, that X is determined independent of Y. Specifically, in the analysis of repeatable events, such as job separations, the missing data will not be MAR after the omission of both left-truncated and fully left-censored cases because the values of X depend on any previous duration values of Y realized for the same subject.

Censoring, therefore, is an important and complicated issue. As stated earlier, however, the issue represents an advantage of event history analysis rather than a disadvantage because event history analysis can handle censored observations adequately in many situations. On the other hand, any simple treatment of right-censored cases, such as omitting the cases from the analysis or assigning an arbitrary value to duration that is larger than the observed value, generates serious bias in parameter estimates (Tuma & Hannan, 1979).

The issue of right censoring may be avoided if a researcher analyzes the determinants of the occurrence versus nonoccurrence of the event within a fixed period of time. For example, by disregarding the duration of nonoccurrence, a researcher may analyze the occurrence versus nonoccurrence of interfirm job separation within the first three years of employment. This analysis is technically adequate[4] if the researcher has a three-year observation period from the beginning of employment for every subject.

However, there are three major limitations for this alternative method. First, the dichotomous distinction for the dependent variable can lead to a great loss of information. Three different kinds of information are lost: (a) variability in the timing of the event among those who had the event within three years, (b) the occurrence and timing of the event for those who had the event after the three-year observation period, and (c) any further duration of employment for those who did not have the event. Second, time-dependent covariates (i.e., explanatory variables whose values vary with time) cannot be employed in the model. Third, and probably most serious, when the effects of covariates on the hazard rate of interfirm job separation vary with time—that is, when interaction effects of covariates and employment duration on the hazard rate exist—the results become conditional upon the length of the arbitrary fixed time period. Then, the effects of covariates on the occurrence versus nonoccurrence of interfirm job separation may change significantly if, for instance, the period of observation is two years instead of three years. Several empirical examples are presented in the following chapters that exhibit the interaction effects of time and covariates on hazard rates. The limitations of the dichotomous distinction for the dependent variable are apparent from these examples.

HAZARD RATE, SURVIVOR FUNCTION, AND LIKELIHOOD FUNCTION

Event history analysis models hazard rates. The hazard rate (or *hazard function*), h(t), expresses the instantaneous risk of having the event at time t, *given that the event did not occur before time t*. The hazard function h(t) is also defined as the ratio of the unconditional instantaneous probability of having the event f(t) divided by the *survival probability* (or *survivor function*) $S(t)$, which is the probability of not having the event prior to time t.

Formally, let T be a random variable for duration of the risk period for an event. Then the hazard rate $h(t)$ is given as

$$h(t) = \lim_{t \to 0} \frac{P(t + \Delta t > T \geq t \mid T \geq t)}{\Delta t} = \frac{f(t)}{S(t)} \tag{1.1}$$

where $P(t + \Delta t > T \geq t \mid T \geq t)$ indicates the probability that the event occurs during the time $(t, t + \Delta t)$ *given that the event did not occur prior to time t*.

The survivor function $S(t)$ is given as

$$S(t) = P(T \geq t) = \exp\left[-\int_0^t h(u)\, du \right] \tag{1.2}$$

The unconditional instantaneous probability of having the event at time t, $f(t)$, which is also called the *probability density function* of T, is given as:

$$f(t) = \lim_{t \to 0} \frac{P(t + \Delta t > T \geq t)}{\Delta t} = h(t) \exp\left[-\int_0^t h(u)\, du \right] \tag{1.3}$$

Generally, if we know one of $h(t)$, $S(t)$, or $f(t)$, we can obtain complete information for the other two (see Kalbfleisch & Prentice, 1980). Hence modeling duration data can be done by specifying the relation between covariates and one of these three functions.

However, in most cases, event history analysis models the hazard rate $h(t)$ rather than $f(t)$ or $S(t)$. There are several reasons for this: (a) It is substantively important to consider the risk attached to a person at a given time, given that the person has not had the event by that time; (b) if such a risk depends on certain time-dependent covariates, it is easy to model the effects of the "current" values of the covariates on hazard rates; and (c) a particular class of models, called *proportional hazards models*, can be employed without specifying a functional form for the effects of time (or duration) on hazard rates. The second point pertains to the fact that if a time-dependent covariate, say $X(t)$, influences $h(t)$, then both $f(t)$ and $S(t)$ depend not only on $X(t)$, but also on previous values of $X(s)$ for $s \leq t$. Without modeling $h(t)$, it is difficult to make a reasonable assumption about the way $f(t)$ or $S(t)$ depends on $X(s)$ for $s \leq t$. The third point pertains to the usefulness of Cox's method, which is discussed in Chapters 5 and 6.

Under the absence of left-censored observations,[5] the likelihood function for a particular set of independent observations of duration $i = 1, \ldots, I$ can be expressed as

$$\prod_{i=1}^{I} h_i(t_i)^{\delta_i} S_i(t_i) \qquad (1.4)$$

where t_i is the duration of the state at risk for the ith sample subject, and δ_i is a dummy variable defined for each observation i to indicate whether the event occurred at time t_i (for which $\delta_i = 1$) or the observation was right censored at time t_i (for which $\delta_i = 0$). Both the hazard function and the survivor function have subscript i because they depend on the values of covariates that are specific to each subject.

Formula 1.4 indicates that for a subject i with an occurrence of the event, his or her contribution to the likelihood function becomes $h_i(t_i)S_i(t_i)$, which is the probability of not having the event between time 0 and time t_i multiplied by the hazard rate of the occurrence of the event at time t_i. This product is simply the probability density function of the occurrence of the event at time t_i, that is, $f_i(t_i)$. For a subject i with a right-censored observation, his or her contribution becomes $S_i(t_i)$, which is the probability of not having the event from between 0 and time t_i. Hence, for subjects with right-censored observations, we can include information about their survival up to the time of censoring without making any assumption about the timing of the event's occurrence in the future.

The maximum likelihood estimates for parameters can be obtained by (a) specifying $h(t)$ as a concrete function of t and (b) obtaining the estimates of the set of parameters that maximizes the likelihood function. Models for $h(t)$ are described in the following chapters.

ORGANIZATION AND CHARACTERISTICS OF THIS BOOK

This book has seven chapters, including this introductory chapter. The following five chapters present three related, but distinct, groups of models and their applications. The last chapter is dedicated to a summary and discussion of issues.

Chapters 2 and 3 present discrete-time logit models and their applications. Discrete-time models are useful when the measurement unit of time is relatively crude, such as year or individual age. A discussion of the analysis of one-way transitions is presented in Chapter 2, and that of two-way transitions in Chapter 3.

Chapter 4 presents log-rate models of continuous-time piecewise constant rates. While the log-rate models have not been widely used, they are important for a basic understanding of multiplicative models of rates, which characterize the models that are introduced in all other chapters of this book.

Chapters 5 and 6 present continuous-time proportional hazards models and related partially parametric models using Cox's partial likelihood method. Applications are presented for these models. Continuous-time models based on maximum likelihood estimation, instead of Cox's method, are also discussed in these two chapters, but no applications are presented. Chapter 6 discusses proportional hazards models, specific nonproportional hazards models, and stratified models. Chapter 7 presents a classification of time-dependent covariates and discusses their uses. Caveats for causal interpretations of their effects in event history analysis are also discussed.

All applications presented in this book are based on the use of programs available in standard statistical packages. The discrete-time logit models are based on the use of the SAS-LOGIST and BMDPLR programs. The log-rate models are based on the use of the SPSS-LOGLINEAR program. The proportional hazards and related models are based on the use of the BMDP2L program. Practical information that is helpful for using these programs is provided in respective chapters. Most of the applications presented in this book permit either complete or partial duplications using the data provided. Each of Chapters 2 through 6 provides exercises for review and practice. These exercises include problems that require replication of some analyses presented in each chapter, as well as some additional problems.

This book has some other major characteristics as well. It focuses on applications more than on a formal presentation of methodology. Hence a discussion of practical, "hands-on" knowledge is emphasized, such as (a) the use and misuse of samples, models, and covariates in applications; (b) the structural arrangement of input data; (c) the specification of various models in particular computer programs; and (d) the interpretation of parameters estimated from models.

This book also emphasizes the importance of modeling from applicative points of view. Generally speaking, I regard good models as those that satisfy three conditions. One condition is fundamental. A model is good only if the statistical assumption of the underlying sampling distribution is adequate for a given data set. Although some issues related to this topic are discussed in this book, its treatment is far from complete. A further discussion of modeling with respect to these issues would require the description of techniques that are beyond the scope of this book.

The second condition is concerned with model selection. Even when a model is adequate regarding the assumption of sampling distribution, it can make less than optimal use of parameters. Hence emphasis is given to selecting a model that accurately and parsimoniously characterizes the relationship between the set of given explanatory variables and hazard rates. While there are many methods of model selection, this book relies on likelihood-ratio and other chi-square tests for comparing nested models. The procedure for model selection and its applications are described for all three groups of methods and models discussed in this book.

Finally, good models are closely related to tests of substantively important hypotheses. The link between the modeling of event history data and the construction of substantive hypotheses is an important topic, but it is often neglected as a nonmethodological issue. However, there is certain general knowledge about the use of event history analysis that helps us to operationalize given substantive hypotheses, or even to identify substantively important hypotheses. This book attempts to provide such knowledge through concrete applications presented in the following five chapters. The applications include empirical research in a variety of substantive areas, including the analysis of interfirm job separation, getting married, dropping out of college, and changes in levels of personal efficacy. In the last chapter, the link between substantive research and the modeling of event history data is summarized and extended.

NOTES

1. However, these two definitions differ slightly. Some rate models may be described adequately as duration models. The Markov process model of transition rates is an example of the latter. See Chapter 3 for a more general case of models that assume truncated duration dependence and do not take duration *fully* into account.

2. Censoring by the termination of observations at a prespecified time, as in the case of censoring by the date of the sample survey, is called *type II* right censoring. On the other hand, censoring by the termination of observations after a prespecified number of events is called *type I* right censoring. Both are examples of *independent censoring* that

can be handled adequately in event history analysis. See Kalbfleisch and Prentice (1980) for further discussion.

3. If we know the initial duration t_{0i} at the beginning of the observation period, we get the conditional likelihood function, given the condition that subject i survived up to time t_{0i}, by replacing survivor probability $S(t_i)$ with the conditional survivor probability $S(t_i)/S(t_{0i})$:

$$S(t_i \mid t_{0i}) = \exp\left[-\int_{t_{0i}}^{t_i} h_i(u)\, du \right]$$

Hence, if we know the value of t_{0i} and all the values of $h_i(t)$ from time t_{0i} to t_i for subject i, we can include the conditional likelihood function for this subject in the analysis.

However, if the hazard rate model includes a random error term for unobserved heterogeneity (which is discussed in Chapter 6), the conditional *marginal* likelihood function cannot be expressed only by information about t_{0i} and $h_i(t)$ from time t_{0i} to t_i for subjects, and requires knowledge of covariates from time 0 to t_{0i}. Hence left truncation cannot be treated adequately under the assumption that the correct model includes a random error term.

4. The use of the complementary log-log function for regression—that is, $\ln[-\ln(1 - P)] = b_0 + \Sigma_i b_i X_i$, where P is the probability of having the event within the fixed period—leads to an estimation of parameters for a proportional hazards model. The use of logistic regression leads to a distinct model, a logit model of the survivor function, but the parameter estimates become similar to those of the complementary log-log model when P is small.

5. See note 4.

2

Discrete-Time Logit Models, I:
The Analysis of
One-Way Transition

METHODS AND MODELS

This chapter and the next describe the use of *discrete-time logit models* for event history analysis. Discrete-time models assume that the event of interest occurs only at discrete time points. In this chapter, the analysis is focused on nonrepeatable one-way transition, that is, transition from one state to another state that occurs at most once for each subject. Nonrepeatable events include such life events as becoming married for the first time, getting the first full-time job, and initiation into marijuana use. The next chapter focuses on the analysis of repeatable one-way and two-way transitions, that is, the analysis of transition from one state to another that can occur more than once for subjects (repeatable one-way transition), and the simultaneous analysis of repeatable transitions from state A to state B and the reverse transition from state B to state A (repeatable two-way transition). Repeatable events include such life events as becoming divorced, having a job separation, and relapse of drug use.

Two major alternatives exist for modeling discrete-time event history data: proportional hazards models and logit models. In this book, I describe only the use of logit models because they can be applied to the data easily using the computer programs of logistic regression that are available from standard statistical packages. If covariates are all categorical, computer programs for log-linear analyses can also be used for logit models. See Kalbfleisch and Prentice (1980) for discrete-time proportional hazards models.

Discrete-time models are used for different reasons. First, discrete-time models can be used to approximate continuous-time models. Although the approximation necessarily introduces bias in parameter estimates, the bias becomes negligible as the conditional probabilities of having the event at discrete time points, given that the event does not occur before each time point, become small. On the other hand, discrete-time models have an advantage over continuous-time models with Cox's method in the handling of ties, as described later.

Other reasons for the use of discrete-time models include situations in which (a) the underlying process is really discrete in time or (b) a binary process that satisfies certain conditions is assumed for a variable obtained from panel data. The latter is discussed in the next chapter.

Reasons for using discrete-time models require different assumptions and thereby different qualifications in their use. In this chapter, I use discrete-time models to approximate continuous-time models. In the next chapter, I discuss their use based on a different assumption.

The discrete-time logit model described in this chapter is based on contributions of Cox (1972) and Brown (1975). A useful discussion of the method is also given by Allison (1982).

In this chapter, models employ *time-dependent covariates*, that is, explanatory variables that vary with time. Some caveats in the use of time-dependent covariates are discussed in this chapter. A more systematic discussion on the use of time-dependent covariates, however, is delayed until Chapter 6. We assume knowledge of the timing of entry into the risk period for all subjects in the sample.

When Is It Appropriate to Use
Discrete-Time Models as an Approximation for
Continuous-Time Models?

Three related considerations are relevant for the use of discrete-time models to approximate continuous-time models. The first pertains to the *unit of time* used for the measurement of the dependent event. Except for surveys that are specially designed for a collection of event history data, the timing of events is seldom measured by a fine time unit. We often have a measurement based on discrete times of fairly large intervals such as year or individual age, instead of a measurement based on year, month, and day. In these cases, it may be more natural to assume a model that reflects a discrete-time measurement.

The second consideration concerns the number of *ties* in the data. Events are tied when two or more subjects in the sample have the event at the same time. Although the underlying continuous-time process has a zero probability of tied events, ties can occur in the data because events are measured at discrete time points. The presence of many ties can lead to a serious bias in parameter estimates when using Cox's method for proportional hazards models, as described in Chapter 6. On the other hand, discrete-time models can handle ties without introducing bias in parameter estimates.

The third and most important consideration pertains to the *adequacy of the approximation* obtained from discrete-time models. This concern is related to the conditional probabilities of having the event at discrete time points. Discrete-time models, both logit and proportional hazards models, are adequate for the approximation of continuous-time models only if the conditional probabilities are reasonably small.[1]

Discrete-Time Models

Suppose T is a discrete random variable that indicates the time of an event. If $T = t$, it means that the event occurs at time t. Suppose that the probability of having an event at t in the population is given by $f(t)$.

$$f(t_i) = P(T = t_i) \qquad i = 1, 2, \ldots \qquad (2.1)$$

where t_i ($i = 1, 2, \ldots$) indicates the ith discrete time point and satisfies $t_1 < t_2 < \ldots$. Then the *survivor function*, $S(t)$, which indicates the probability of *not* having the event prior to time t, is given as

$$S(t_i) = P(T \geq t_i) = \sum_{j \geq i} f(t_j) \qquad (2.2)$$

The hazard at t_i is defined as the *conditional probability* of having the event at t_i, given that the event did not occur prior to time t_i, such that

$$\lambda_i = P(T = t_i \mid T \geq t_i) = f(t_i)/S(t_i) \qquad (2.3)$$

Then, we also obtain

$$S(t_i) = \prod_{j=1}^{i-1} (1 - \lambda_j) \qquad (2.4)$$

Any parametric specification of conditional probabilities for λ_j, $j = 1$, 2, ... becomes a discrete-time hazard model.

Discrete-Time Logit Model
(Owing to Brown, 1975; Cox, 1972)

The discrete-time logit model is defined using the concept of a logit, or log-odds. The *odds* are simply the ratio of two probabilities for any mutually exclusive states. In particular, $P/(1 - P)$ defines the odds for a given probability P. *Logit* is the log-odds of P—that is, $\ln[P/(1 - P)]$—using the natural base of the logarithm.

In the discrete-time logit model, the odds for conditional probabilities are modeled. The basic model assumes that for any person *in the population* the odds of having the event at each discrete-time t_i, $i = 1$, $2, \ldots$, are proportional to the odds of having the event for some specific persons who represent the set of *baseline states* of covariates, such that

$$\frac{\lambda(t_i ; X)}{1 - \lambda(t_i ; X)} = \frac{\lambda_0(t_i)}{1 - \lambda_0(t_i)} \exp\left(\sum_k b_k X_k\right) \qquad (2.5)$$

where $\lambda(t_i ; X)$ is the conditional probability of having the event at time t_i for a given covariate vector $X = (X_1, \ldots, X_K)$, and b_k, $k = 1, \ldots, K$ are parameters. The *baseline hazard function*, $\lambda_0(t_i)$, $i = 1, \ldots, I$, is characterized by conditional probabilities for cases in which the covariate vector $X = 0$. Formula 2.5 also implies that the odds of having the event at each discrete time point are $\exp(\Sigma_k b_k X_k)$ times higher for subjects characterized by covariates X compared with subjects in the baseline group. The model also indicates that, controlling for other covariates, an increase in one unit of X_k increases (or decreases) the odds of having the event $\exp(b_k)$ times.

As the measurement of time becomes finer and finer, the ratio of two odds—that is, $\{\lambda(t_i ; X)/[1 - \lambda(t_i ; X)]\}/\{\lambda_0(t_i)/[1 - \lambda_0(t_i)]\}$—approaches the ratio of two rates—$\lambda(t_i ; X)/\lambda_0(t_i)$—and therefore we obtain a continuous-time proportional hazards model. (See Chapters 4 and 5 for a description of continuous-time proportional hazards models.) Hence, when the conditional probabilities are sufficiently small, the logit model provides an approximation to the continuous-time proportional hazards model.

Formula 2.5 can be expressed in a logistic regression form as follows:

$$\ln\left\{\lambda(t_i ; X)/[1 - \lambda(t_i ; X)]\right\} = a_i + \sum_k b_k X_k \qquad (2.6)$$

where a_i is equal to $\ln\{\lambda_0(t_i)/[1 - \lambda_0(t_i)]\}$, that is, the log-odds for the baseline group.

If covariates X are all *time-independent* (i.e., they do not vary with time), we have a *proportional odds model*. In this model, the odds of having an event—that is, $\lambda(t_i; X)/[1 - \lambda(t_i; X)]$—form a constant ratio with respect to time among groups that are distinguished by the covariates. In this respect the proportional odds model is similar to the proportional hazards model described in Chapters 4 and 5: While the ratio of odds is time-constant for the former, the ratio of rates is time-constant for the latter. (For more about proportional odds models for duration data, see Cox & Oakes, 1984.) We can also test *nonproportional odds models* by using *time-dependent covariates* $X(t)$. The time-dependent covariates may include interaction effects of time and covariates, as described later.

In some cases, a parametric modeling of time effects may be employed. The model that replaces a_i by at_i or $a\ln(t_i)$ in Formula 2.6 is similar to the Gompertz and Weibull models, respectively, which will be discussed in Chapter 4. The linear time trend or the log-linear time trend is hypothesized for the log-odds of conditional probabilities instead of log-rates, and is defined for discrete time points.

A practical advantage of the discrete-time logit model compared with the discrete-time proportional hazards model is that we can use a logistic regression program for estimating parameters. The structure of the input data, however, differs between the conventional logistic regression analysis and the use of logistic regression for the analysis of discrete-time event history data. While the former uses one observation for each sample subject, the latter uses multiple observations for each. Accordingly, the input data for the logistic regression must be arranged in a specific way, as described later.

Chi-Square Tests and Comparisons of Nested Models

Chi-square tests and their use for model selection are described below. For discrete-time logit models, we need to distinguish when aggregate versus person-period data are used as input. We may obtain two different values of likelihood-ratio chi-square statistics depending on the input data and computer programs.

The likelihood-ratio chi-square for goodness-of-fit tests, G^2, is available when the input data are *cross-classified frequency data*. It is calculated as follows:

$$G^2 = 2\sum_i f_i \ln(f_i / F_i) \tag{2.7}$$

where f_i is the observed aggregate-level frequency of events for state i, and F_i is the corresponding frequency *expected* from the model. A set of states $i, i = 1, \ldots$ represents cross-classified categories of discrete-time points and categorical states of covariates. This chi-square statistic represents the deviation of a set of frequencies expected from the model from a set of observed frequencies. Hence a larger value for a given degrees of freedom indicates a poorer fit of the model with the data. The statistical insignificance of G^2 indicates that the null hypothesis that the observed frequency data are generated from the model cannot be rejected. The statistic G^2 can be also expressed as

$$\begin{aligned} G^2 = 2[&(\log - \text{likelihood of the } \textit{saturated model}) \\ &- (\log - \text{likelihood of the tested model})] \end{aligned} \tag{2.8}$$

where the saturated model uses as many parameters as the number of cells of cross-classified frequency data and, thereby, has expected frequencies identical to observed frequencies. (See Chapter 4 for more about the saturated model.) The values of G^2 are available from some logistic regression programs when the aggregate-level input data are used, such as BMDPLR, as well as from log-linear programs (such as SPSS-LOGLINEAR and SAS-CATMOD).

Another likelihood-ratio chi-square, L^2, can be obtained when person-period input data are used (described later). The statistic L^2 is given as:

$$\begin{aligned} L^2 = 2 [&(\log - \text{likelihood of the tested model}) \\ &- (\log - \text{likelihood of } \textit{constant rate} \text{ model})] \end{aligned} \tag{2.9}$$

where the constant rate model includes only the parameter for the intercept. Hence the statistic L^2 provides a significance test for a set of parameters used in the model, excluding the intercept. A larger value of L^2 for a given degrees of freedom indicates a greater significance level. The statistical insignificance of L^2 indicates that the tested model is not significantly better than the constant rate model. Programs SAS-LOGIST and SPSS-LOGISTIC REGRESSION (but not SPSSX-PROBIT) provides L^2. BMDPLR provides the value of the log-likelihood from which we can calculate L^2.

As can be seen from Formulas 2.8 and 2.9, for a particular model under consideration the two chi-square statistics differ only with respect to the comparative model. Both likelihood-ratio statistics, G^2 and L^2, can be used for comparisons of *nested models*. The tests are equivalent because $G_1{}^2 - G_2{}^2 = L_2{}^2 - L_1{}^2$ holds true between nested models 1 and 2. Two models are nested if and only if one model is obtained by adding some parameter(s) to the other model. The likelihood-ratio test for comparing nested models assumes that the model with more parameters is the correct model. While this assumption is difficult to examine with L^2 because L^2 does not provide a measure for the fit of the model with the data, the adequacy of this assumption can be examined with G^2. Generally, using G^2 to compare nested models is adequate only if the model with a smaller G^2 value fits the data.

In this chapter, only the likelihood-ratio test is used for model selection. Although model selection can be based on a different procedure that permits comparisons among nonnested models, such as the AIC (Akaike, 1974; Sakamoto, Ishiguro, & Kitagawa, 1986) and BIC (Raftery, 1986; see also Heckman & Walker, 1987; Schwarz, 1978) procedures, they are not employed here. The likelihood-ratio test for comparing nested models tests the null hypothesis that expected values from the models are identical except for differences due to random variation. It follows that if the difference in chi-square between two nested models is significant for a given difference in the degrees of freedom, we should reject the null hypothesis and conclude that the model that has more parameters improves the fit of the model with fewer parameters. On the other hand, if the difference in chi-square is insignificant, we cannot reject the null hypothesis. Then we should accept the model with fewer parameters as having a more parsimonious fit with the data than the model with more parameters.

Construction of Input Data

In the use of discrete-time logit models, the construction of input data becomes a major practical task. The following sections describe two alternative ways to construct the input data: individual-level (person-period) and aggregate-level data.

Use of a Person-Period Record File

If several time-dependent covariates are included in the model, the easiest way to generate the input data is to have a person-period record file. For each sample subject and for each discrete time point at which the subject is at risk for having the event, the file contains information about the occurrence or nonoccurrence of the event in ques-

Table 2.1

A Person-Age Record File

ID	AGE	RACE	EDUC	MS	ID	AGE	RACE	EDUC	MS
1	13	0	1	0	3	13	0	1	0
1	14	0	1	0	3	14	0	1	0
1	15	0	1	0	3	15	0	1	0
1	16	0	1	0	3	16	0	1	0
1	17	0	1	0	3	17	0	1	0
1	18	0	2	0	3	18	0	0	0
1	19	0	2	0	3	19	0	0	0
1	20	0	2	0	3	20	0	2	0
1	21	0	2	0	3	21	0	2	1
1	22	0	2	0	4	13	0	1	0
1	23	0	2	0	4	14	0	1	0
2	13	1	1	0	4	15	0	1	0
2	14	1	1	0	4	16	0	0	0
2	15	1	1	0	4	17	0	0	0
2	16	1	1	0	4	18	0	0	0
2	17	1	1	0	4	19	0	0	0
2	18	1	0	0	4	20	0	0	1
2	19	1	0	1	5	.	.	.	.

tion as well as the values of time-dependent and time-independent covariates.

Table 2.1 presents a hypothetical example of a person-age record file for the analysis of getting married. It is assumed here that all subjects enter the risk period at age 13. For simplicity, assume that the file has five variables—ID, AGE, RACE, EDUC, and MS—defined as follows. ID distinguishes different subjects by a sequential number; AGE indicates chronological age; RACE is a dummy variable that distinguishes two racial groups; EDUC is a time-varying variable for participation in full-time schooling, which takes 1 for secondary education, 2 for postsecondary education, and 0 for the state of not being in school full-time; and MS is marital status, which takes 0 for the period of being single prior to marriage and 1 for age at marriage.

In the analysis of getting married, all age periods prior to marriage (for age 13 and after) and age at marriage are included in the file. All other age periods are omitted from the file. If the single period is censored, the file includes records up to the age of censoring. In Table 2.1, the first subject (ID = 1) is age 23 at the time of the survey and has never married. Hence his or her records for MS always take the value 0. Records for the other three subjects (ID = 2, 3, 4) are terminated at the occurrence of marriage, at ages 19, 21, and 20, respectively. The variable MS is used as the dependent variable for the logistic regression. The time-varying variable EDUC may be used to reflect a categorical distinction in the three education states by converting it into a pair of dummy variables. It may also be used to create another dummy variable such as the before/after distinction in first leaving full-time schooling.

Similarly, in the analysis of divorce based on person-age records, subjects enter the risk period at their age of marriage. They remain at risk up to either the age of divorce or the age of censoring. In this case, the age of entry into the risk set varies with subjects. It is important to include in the file a variable for the duration of marriage because hazard-rate models use this variable as the time variable. However, age itself can be used as a time-dependent covariate of the hazard rate of divorce.

Researchers who wish to distinguish *competing events* should assign a distinct code for each type of event. For instance, competing events may be defined for distinct types of interfirm job separations, such as voluntary and involuntary separations, or for distinct transitions from the state of unmarried cohabitation, such as separation from the partner and marriage to the partner. A particular code can be treated as an occurrence of the event, while other codes are treated as censored observations. A further discussion about competing events appears in Chapter 7.

Although the person-period record file is very useful, there are several potential disadvantages for its use compared with the use of aggregate input data, which is described below. First, the person-period record file can be huge and very costly to use. If there are 2,000 subjects, and each has an average of 50 time points within his or her risk period, then the file would contain 100,000 records. One way to reduce computer time and costs is to use conventional linear regression with OLS estimation procedure for the dependent 0-1 variable with person-period data during preliminary exploratory analysis, then use the logistic regression only for a select set of models in the final analysis. Second, the creation of a person-period record file may be time-consuming if researchers wish to include in the file all potential dependent and independent variables for the analysis. Hence the use of aggregate frequency data as input data may become a time-saving alternative, although it is practical only for situations with only a few time-dependent covariates.

Third, the aggregate frequency data as input data provide the likelihood-ratio chi-square G^2 for the goodness-of-fit test of models with data.

Construction of Aggregate Input Data

Many programs for logistic regression permit records to be weighted by the number of observations. Hence the use of aggregate frequency data as input data for discrete-time logit models is feasible. The construction of such frequency input data is especially sensible for models in which (a) there are few or no time-dependent covariates, and (b) all covariates, including time-independent covariates, are categorical and the number of combinations for the time variable and the covariates is much smaller than the number of person-period records. The procedure for calculating aggregate input data is described below. The procedure can be easily programmed by SAS and linked to the SAS or BMDP programs.

The procedure for cases with a single time-dependent covariate is described below. This procedure can be generalized easily to include a few time-dependent covariates. However, it is rather impractical to use the procedure for data with more than a few time-dependent covariates. The following steps need to be done. Suppose N time-independent covariates and one time-dependent covariate, X, are used in the analysis.

Step 1. Sort the individual data by the N time-independent covariates.

Step 2. Do the procedure described in Figure 2.1 for *each* segment of the sorted data within which the time-independent covariates do not change their values.

Step 3. At each point of change in the time-independent covariates' values, output to a new file a record that includes the following: (a) the number of events at time t and at state k of variable X [#EVENTS$_k(t)$]; (b) the number of persons at risk at time t and state k [#RISK$_k(t)$]; (c) the value of time t; (d) the state k of variable X, for all $t = 1, \ldots, T$ and all $k = 1, \ldots, K$; and (e) the values of all the N time-independent covariates. Thus one record in the new file has $4TK + N$ variables.

Step 4. Read the file created in Step 3 and arrange the data in the following way. For each record, output to a new file the following pair of records *separately for each distinct time t and each distinct*

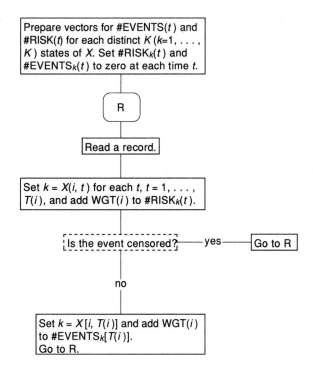

Figure 2.1. Procedure to Calculate $\#EVENTS_k(t)$ and $\#RISK_k(t)$ When a Time-Dependent Covariate $X(i, t)$ Has K States

NOTES: $WGT(i)$: individual sampling weight for the ith person (if any); $= 1$ if not otherwise specified. $T(i)$: time at which the observation is terminated for the ith person. $X(i, t)$: the particular state of X for the ith person at time t.

state k of X. Each old record thus generates a maximum of $2TK$ new records. Each new record will have three major variables (DEP, OBS, TIME) plus the $N + 1$ covariates including X, as defined below. The new variable DEP is assigned 1 for occurrences of the event and 0 for nonoccurrences.

Record 1 for each t: DEP = 1, TIME = t, OBS = $\#EVENTS_k(t)$.
Record 2 for each t: DEP = 0, TIME = t, OBS = $\#RISK_k(t) - \#EVENTS_k(t)$.

In order to reduce the number of records, the output file may include only cases where OBS > 0.

In applying a logistic regression analysis to the aggregate data, we use DEP and OBS, respectively, as the dependent variable and the weight for records.

SOME MISUSES OF COVARIATES IN LIFE-COURSE RESEARCH

In this chapter, I present an analysis of getting married with substantive hypotheses related to life-course research. The sections following present discussions of two misuses of covariates in life-course research. These discussions apply to hazard-rate models in general.

A Misuse of Life-Course Characteristics in Predicting a Life Event

The principle discussed here is simple: Do not make a time-independent characterization for life-course transitions that are realized during the period of risk.

Researchers who analyze event history data will be interested in the interdependence of life events. However, one possible misuse of covariates occurs in predicting the occurrence of a life event when researchers employ a *time-independent* characterization of "life-course covariates" that are in fact time dependent.

Suppose a researcher includes in the model for the hazard rates of becoming divorced a time-independent covariate that distinguishes whether or not the subject had a child during marriage. This covariate is highly likely to have a negative coefficient, seemingly indicating that those who had a child in marriage are less likely to become divorced. The model, however, is completely misspecified. The negative coefficient is obtained not because of the causal interpretation given above, but because subjects with a longer duration of marriage have a longer risk period for having a child in marriage. Hence the dependent variable—that is, the duration of marriage—affects the covariate's value. How can we solve the problem? The only solution is to distinguish between having a child and not having a child as states of a time-dependent covariate. If the survey does not have a measurement on the timing of childbirth, then researchers cannot use childbirth as a predictor of divorce.

Generally speaking, life-course characteristics can be used as time-independent covariates for the occurrence of an event if and only if the covariates reflect a subject state *prior to entering the risk period.* In predicting divorce, for example, one can legitimately include whether or not subjects have a premarital birth. On the other hand, all the life-course states that can change after entry into the risk period must be characterized as the states of time-dependent covariates—unless they are defined as states found at the time of entry into the risk period, such as the level of education at the time of marriage in predicting divorce.

A Misuse in the Distinction
Between Before and After the Occurrence of
a Transition as a Time-Dependent Covariate

The second principle for the proper use of covariates of life-course characteristics is also simple: Do not define a time-dependent covariate as a before/after distinction for the *last* occurrence of a particular life-course transition.

One can misuse even time-dependent covariates in characterizing different life-course states. Many cross-sectional surveys collect data regarding when subjects *first* enter into or exit from a particular state, such as the timing of first employment and the timing of the first exit from full-time schooling. Surveys also collect data on when subjects *last* enter into or exit from a particular state, such as the timing of the last exit from full-time schooling. Without detailed life-history data, one may wish to define a time-dependent predictor as a subject's condition before and after a particular life-course transition. For example, time-dependent predictors of marriage may include entry into employment or exit from schooling.

In order to construct time-dependent covariates that distinguish before and after a particular transition, one can use data on the first occurrence of life-course transitions. However, the use of covariates that are based on the last occurrence of transitions generates bias in parameter estimates. This bias occurs because values of a covariate that distinguish before and after the last occurrence of life-course transitions depend on the timing of censoring by the survey. This violates the assumption of independence between covariate values and the censoring time.

Figure 2.2 illustrates how values of two variables, XF and XL, are coded for two distinct censoring times. The solid line indicates the

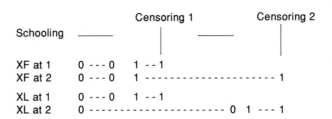

Figure 2.2. Variables and Censoring
NOTE: XF is the covariate for "before and after the first exit from school."

period of schooling; variable XF codes each period as the subject's condition before (XF = 0) and after (XF = 1) the first exit from school, and XL codes each period as the subject's condition before (XL = 0) and after (XL = 1) the last exit from school. The figure clearly indicates that while there is no change in the values of XF for different censoring times, the values of XL change if the period of observation is extended and there is another period of schooling. This example demonstrates that while XF's values are independent of censoring, XL's values are not.

APPLICATION:
AN ANALYSIS OF THE TIMING OF MARRIAGE

Data and Covariates

Below I use data for males aged 25-64 in the 1973 Occupational Changes in a Generation Survey. The survey is a replication of the 1962 survey that was analyzed by Blau and Duncan (1967). Major results for the analysis of the 1973 survey are reported by Featherman and Hauser (1978). Hogan (1978) used this survey data set in a study that is substantively related to the one presented here.

The survey contains data on the age of subjects at marriage, at first employment, and at the survey date. The analysis presented below focuses on the determinants of the timing of marriage. As covariates, I include (a) age as the time variable; (b) a set of dummy variables for the age of employment as time-dependent covariates, using the state of before employment as the baseline state; and (c) time-independent covariates for the distinction in age cohorts. To simplify the analysis, control variables other than age cohorts are omitted. A preliminary study (not reported) indicates that the inclusion of some time-independent covariates other than age cohorts does not change the results significantly.

The aggregate input data for the logistic regression are generated in SAS by the procedure described in Figure 2.1.

Substantive Hypotheses

The normative timing of life events and the normative sequencing among life events have been studied in life-course research (e.g., Hogan, 1978, 1981; Mare, Winship, & Kubitschek, 1984; Marini, 1984a, 1984b; Riley, Johnson, & Fones, 1972). These normative expectations, however, can conflict with one another. In the analysis presented here, three hypotheses are tested that are related to the relationship between the timing of first employment and the timing of marriage. Hogan's (1978) study indicates that a normative sequence exists whereby subjects move from schooling to work and then to marriage. This analysis is concerned with the determinants of the timing of marriage, which is believed to satisfy both the requirement for normative timing, whereby marriage ought to occur at certain ages, and the requirement for normative sequencing, such that marriage ought to occur after employment. Three hypotheses are constructed.

In order to satisfy the sequencing norm, subjects will be less likely to get married before they are employed. Hence the first hypothesis:

• *Hypothesis 1:* Controlling for age, "ever had an employment" as a time-dependent covariate increases the hazard rate of getting married.

However, if subjects postpone marriage because they have not yet started to work, they create an increasing risk for violating the normative timing (i.e., age) of marriage. Some subjects may consider the violation of the normative sequence of marriage as less undesirable than the violation of the normative timing of marriage. As age increases, they may decide to marry prior to starting work so as not to violate the normative timing of marriage. Hence we can expect the following:

• *Hypothesis 2:* The effect of "ever had an employment" on increasing the rate of getting married will decrease with age.

Other people may consider the violation of the normative timing of marriage less undesirable than the violation of the normative sequence of marriage. Those people will postpone marriage until they start to work. Once they satisfy the sequencing norm, however, they may also wish to satisfy the timing norm. But as the age at which they start work increases, fewer years remain to satisfy the normative timing of marriage. Accordingly, the timing of marriage may be accelerated further during the remaining ages. Hence we can expect:

- *Hypothesis 3:* As the age of employment increases, the effect of "ever had an employment" in accelerating the timing of marriage will become stronger, controlling for age.

Tests of these three hypotheses are presented below, along with a detailed analysis related to the tests.

Programming of Models

The discrete-time logit model can be applied by using any logistic regression program. I use SAS-LOGIST below because it is useful for testing models of interest in the present analysis, which include categorical age effects combined with interaction effects of linear age and covariates.[2]

Table 2.2 presents a sample SAS program that illustrates the definition of variables and the use of SAS-LOGIST. The function of the program is as follows. Lines 2-9 describe the variables stored in the input SAS data file, lines 10-48 define covariates, and the last four lines (49-52) specify a logistic regression model to be applied to the data.

In lines 13 to 18, a set of three dummy variables for the categorical expression of cohorts is derived from the interval-scale cohort variable CHT. Lines 19-24 define a set of six age-of-employment dummy variables using the variable EMPAGE. The state of "before employment" is the baseline state. Using the set of age-of-employment dummy variables, two variables, U_EMP and L_EMP, are defined in lines 25 and 26. The variable U_EMP represents the *uniform* effect of "after employment" compared with "before employment." The variable L_EMP, when it is simultaneously used with U_EMP in the model, represents a *linear* effect of the age of employment among states of "after employment." Employment ages under 17 are used as the baseline state for L_EMP.

Table 2.2
A Sample SAS Program

	Line[a]
DATA IPTDT;	1
SET SASFILE.MRG;	2
/* THE INPUT FILE HAS VARIABLES CHT AGE EMPAGE FREQ EVT.	3
CHT: AGE COHORT IN 1973: 0:25-34; 1:35-44; 2:45-54; 3:55-64	4
AGE: AGE, 13-40	5
EMPAGE: 0:BEFORE EMPLOYMENT; 1: FIRST EMPLOYMENT UNDER 17;	6
2: 18-19; 3:20-21; 4:22-23; 5:24-25; 6: 25 AND OVER.	7
FREQ: FFREQUENCY THAT EACH RECORD REPRESENTS	8
EVT: 1:OCCURRENCE; 0: NON-OCCURRENCE */	9
ARRAY AGEDMY{14} AGEDMY1-AGEDMY14;	10
ARRAY EMPDMY{6} EMPDMY1-EMPDMY6;	11
ARRAY INTDMY{14} INTDMY1-INTDMY14;	12
CHT1=0;	13
CHT2=0;	14
CHT3=0;	15
IF CHT=1 THEN CHT1=1;	16
IF CHT=2 THEN CHT2=1; ˙	17
IF CHT=3 THEN CHT3=1;	18
DO I=1 TO 6;	19
EMPDMY{I}=0;	20
END;	21
DO I=1 TO 6;	22
IF EMPAGE=I THEN EMPDMY{I}=1;	23
END;	24
U_EMP=EMPDMY1+EMPDMY2+EMPDMY3+EMPDMY4+EMPDMY5+	25
EMPDMY6;	
L_EMP=EMPDMY2+EMPDMY3*2+EMPDMY4*3+EMPDMY5*4+EMPDMY6*5;	26
DO I=1 TO 14;	27
AGEDMY{I}=0;	28
END;	29
DO I=1 TO 14;	30
I1=13+(I-1)*2;	31
I2=I1+1;	32
IF AGE=I1 OR AGE=I2 THEN AGEDMY{I}=1;	33
END;	34
DO I=1 to 14;	35
INTDMY{I}=U_EMP*AGEDMY{I};	36
END;	37
INTDMY9_14=INTDMY9+INTDMY10+INTDMY11+INTDMY12+	38
INTDMY13+INTDMY14;	
L_AGE=0;	39
DO I=1 TO 14;	40
L_AGE=L_AGE+AGEDMY{I}*(I-7)*2;	41
END;	42

Continued

Table 2.2, Continued

L_AGE=L_AGE-1;	43
Q_AGE=L_AGE**2;	44
INT_UL=U_EMP*L_AGE;	45
INT_UQ=U_EMP*Q_AGE;	46
INT_LL=L_EMP*L_AGE;	47
INT_LQ=L_EMP*Q_AGE;	48
PROC LOGIST DATA=IPTDT PCOV;	49
WEIGHT FREQ;	50
MODEL EVT=AGEDMY1-AGEDMY4 AGEDMY6-AGEDMY14 CHT1-CHT3	51
U_EMP L_EMP INTDMY1-INTDMY4 INTDMY6-INTDMY8 INTDMY9_14;	52

NOTE: a. Line numbers do not appear in the program.

In lines 27 to 34, a set of 14 dummy variables for age are defined according to the values of AGE. Each dummy variable represents a two-year interval within the age period 13-40. For example, AGEDMY1 represents ages 13-14, and AGEDMY28 represents ages 39-40. Lines 35 to 37 define the interactions between dummy variables for age and the uniform effect of after employment (U_EMP). Line 38 defines INTDMY9_14 by combining the interaction terms for the last six age periods. Lines 39-43 are used for the linear effect of age (L_AGE), which is (a) defined at two-year intervals, and (b) scaled to vary from −13 (for ages 13-14) to +13 (for ages 39-40). Its value is calculated as the midpoint of the two-year age interval minus 26.5. Line 44 defines the quadratic term for age. Finally, lines 45-48 define four interaction variables as the interactions between the linear and quadratic terms of age and the uniform and linear terms of age of employment.

All models that are tested in this chapter can be described using the variables defined in lines 10-48 of Table 2.2. However, each particular model uses only a subset of these variables.

Lines 49-52 give an example of how to specify the logistic regression model in SAS-LOGIST. PROC LOGIST calls a logistic regression program; DATA specifies where the input data are stored; PCOV causes the variance-covariance matrix of parameter estimates to be output; and the WEIGHT statement, WEIGHT = FREQ, specifies that each record represents the number of cases that variable FREQ provides.

The MODEL statement indicates the dependent variable and its covariates. The variable on the left-hand side of the equation is the dependent (0-1) variable, and those on the right-hand side of the equation are covariates. The model specified here corresponds to Model 13, which appears in Tables 2.3 and 2.4. All other models that appear in Tables 2.3 and 2.4 were estimated by substituting another set of covariates in the MODEL statement.

Comparison of Models Using Likelihood-Ratio Tests

A total of 14 models are tested. Their likelihood-ratio test statistics, L^2, are presented in Table 2.3. Comparisons between nested models, based on the difference in L^2, are also given in Table 2.3. Parameter estimates for selected models are given in Table 2.4.

There is one limitation in the analysis presented here. In order to simplify the presentation of the illustrative analysis, interaction effects between age cohorts and other variables are not modeled, and only the main effects for age cohorts are included in the models. On the other hand, interaction effects for both age and age-of-employment variables are explored. These effects have direct relevance for the test of the hypotheses described earlier.

Panel I of Table 2.3 presents the results of two proportional odds models, that is, models that do not include any interaction effects of time (age) and other covariates: Model 1 specifies age and cohort effects, while Model 2 specifies age, cohort, and age-of-employment effects. A comparison of Models 1 and 2 shows that the inclusion of time-dependent covariates, to distinguish before and after the first employment for different ages of employment, significantly improves the fit of the model with the data.

Panel II of Table 2.3 presents the results from three proportional odds models that are modifications of Model 2. The results from Model 2 show a curvilinear shape for age effects (see Table 2.4). Model 3 replaces the categorical effects of age that are included in Model 2 with linear and quadratic effects of age. Since scores of L_AGE and Q_AGE are defined for the 14 age categories used in Model 2, Models 2 and 3 are nested. Their comparison in Panel II of Table 2.3 indicates that Model 3, which employs a parametric characterization for age effects, attains a significantly worse fit than Model 2. Model 4 hypothesizes the uniform effect of "ever had an employment" among different ages of employment (U_EMP). This model is also significantly worse in fit than Model 2. However, Model 5, which includes both the uniform effect and the linear effect of the age of employment (i.e., U_EMP and L_EMP), is a more parsimoniously fitting model than Model 2.

Table 2.3

Comparison of Models Based on Likelihood-Ratio Tests

	L^2	df	P
I. Two Basic Proportional Odds Models			
Model 1: Age and Cohort Effects (Categorical)	16618.16	16	.000
Model 2: Age, Cohort, Employment Effects	19125.41	22	.000
Model 2 vs. Model 1	2507.25	6	.000
II. Modification of Model 2: Proportional Odds Models			
Model 3: Curvilinear Age Effects	17912.49	11	.000
Model 4: Uniform Employment Effect (U_EMP)	19101.32	17	.000
Model 5: Uniform & Linear Employment Effect (U_EMP & L_EMP)	19121.27	18	.000
Model 2 vs. Model 3	1212.92	11	.000
Model 2 vs. Model 4	24.09	5	.000
Model 2 vs. Model 5	4.14	4	> .500
III. Modification of Model 5: Nonproportional Odds Models			
Model 6: plus U-EMP*L_AGE (L_AGE is a linear effect of age)	19314.36	19	.000
Model 7: plus U_EMP*L_AGE, L_EMP*L_AGE	19318.26	20	.000
Model 8: plus U_EMP*L_AGE, U_EMP*(L_AGE)^2	19471.74	20	.000
Model 9: plus U_EMP*L_AGE, U_EMP*(L_AGE)^2, L_EMP*L_AGE	19472.62	21	.000
Model 10: plus U_EMP*L_AGE, U_EMP*(L_AGE)^2, L_EMP*L_AGE, L_EMP*(L_AGE)^2	19473.89	22	.000
Model 11: plus U_EMP*AGE	19533.32	31	.000
Model 12: plus U_EMP*AGE, L_EMP*AGE[a]	19545.16	42	.000
Model 13: last six interactions collapsed for Model 10.	19525.68	26	.000
Model 14: U_EMP and L_EMP replaced by categories in Model 13	19529.06	30	.000
Model 6 vs. Model 5	193.09	1	.000
Model 7 vs. Model 6	3.90	1	< .050
Model 8 vs. Model 6	157.38	1	.000
Model 9 vs. Model 8	0.88	1	> .300
Model 10 vs. Model 8	2.15	2	> .100
Model 11 vs. Model 8	61.58	11	.000
Model 12 vs. Model 11	11.94	11	> .300
Model 11 vs. Model 13	7.64	5	> .100
Model 14 vs. Model 13	3.38	4	> .400

NOTE: a. L_EMP*AGE has only 11 degrees of freedom because it is collinear with U_EMP*AGE under age 17 (i.e., for ages 13-14, 15-16).

Table 2.4

An Analysis of Getting Married: Men Aged 25-64 in the 1973
Occupational Change in a Generation Survey

Covariates	Model 1	Model 2	Model 5	Model 8	Model 13	Model 14
			Logistic Regression Results			
I-1. Time-Varying Age (versus 21-22)						
13-14	-4.440***	-3.990***	-3.989***	-4.471***	-4.590***	-4.590***
15-16	-3.816***	-3.460***	-3.459***	-3.965***	-4.311***	-4.310***
17-18	-1.792***	-1.617***	-1.611***	-2.040***	-2.261***	-2.261***
19-20	-0.605***	-0.539***	-0.536***	-0.749***	-0.868***	-0.868***
21-22	[0.000]	[0.000]	[0.000]	[0.000]	[0.000]	[0.000]
23-24	0.194***	0.128***	0.131***	0.310***	0.199***	0.199***
25-26	0.247***	0.132***	0.135***	0.448***	0.269***	0.269***
27-28	0.183***	0.039	0.042	0.428***	0.221***	0.220**
29-30	0.040	-0.117**	-0.114**	0.277***	-0.088	-0.089
31-32	-0.190***	-0.353***	-0.350***	-0.027	-0.321***	-0.322***
33-34	-0.442***	-0.608***	-0.605***	-0.425***	-0.576***	-0.577***
35-36	-0.568***	-0.736***	-0.732***	-0.770***	-0.703***	-0.703***
37-38	-0.836***	-0.900***	-0.897***	-1.230***	-0.869***	-0.869***
39-40	-0.969***	-1.131***	-1.128***	-1.836***	-1.099***	-1.099***
II. Age Cohort (versus 25-34 in 1973)						
35-44	-0.172***	-0.178***	-0.178***	-0.186***	-0.186***	-0.185***
45-54	-0.345***	-0.366***	-0.367***	-0.373***	-0.372***	-0.370***
55-64	-0.559***	-0.597***	-0.600***	-0.603***	-0.601***	-0.598***
III-1. The Age of the First Employment (Time-dependent; vs. Before Employment)						
Under 17	—	0.715***	—	—	—	0.489***
17-18	—	0.775***	—	—	—	0.572***
19-20	—	0.760***	—	—	—	0.592***
21-22	—	0.797***	—	—	—	0.659***
23-24	—	0.881***	—	—	—	0.744***
25 and over	—	0.879***	—	—	—	0.731***
III-2. The Age of the First Employment (Time-dependent; vs. Before Employment)						
U_EMP	—	—	0.722***	0.228***	0.501***	—
L_EMP[a]	—	—	0.031***	0.052***	0.053***	—
IV-1 Interaction with Linear and Quadratic Effects of Age						
U_EMP*L_AGE[b]—	—	—	—	-0.0370***	—	—
U_EMP*(L-AGE)²—	—	—	—	0.0098***	—	—
IV-2 Interaction with Categorical Effects of Age (versus 21-22)						
U_EMP*[13-14] —	—	—	—	—	1.869***	1.880***
U_EMP*[15-16] —	—	—	—	—	1.712***	1.723***
U_EMP*[17-18] —	—	—	—	—	1.003***	1.000***
U_EMP*[19-20] —	—	—	—	—	0.470***	0.469***
U_EMP*[21-22] —	—	—	—	—	[0.000]	[0.000]

Continued

Table 2.4, Continued

			Logistic Regression Results			
Covariates	Model 1	Model 2	Model 5	Model 8	Model 13	Model 14
U_EMP*[23-24]	—	—	—	—	-0.078	-0.082
U_EMP*[25-26]	—	—	—	—	-0.148[*]	-0.148[*]
U_EMP*[27-28]	—	—	—	—	-0.191[*]	-0.188[*]
U_EMP*[29-40]	—	—	—	—	-0.012	-0.007
V. Intercept	-1.531[***]	-2.042[***]	-2.045[***]	-2.011[***]	-1.898[***]	-1.899[***]

NOTES: a. L_EMP takes 0 for the age of employment that is under 17, 1 for 17-18, 2 for 19-20, 3 for 21-22, 5 for 23-24, and 6 for 25 and over.
b. L_AGE takes a midpoint value of age minus 26.5 for each two-year interval and varies from -13 to 13.

Panel III of Table 2.3 presents several models that modify Model 5. Models 6-12 test interaction effects of age and U_EMP and of age and L_EMP, searching for the most parsimonious characterization of the interaction effects. The interaction effect of age and L_EMP weakly exists when only the interaction effect of linear age and U_EMP are simultaneously taken into account (Model 7 versus Model 6). However, the effect disappears when we also take into account the interaction effect of quadratic age and U_EMP (Model 9 versus Model 8). The insignificance of the interaction effects of L_EMP and age is also confirmed by treating age categorically (Model 12 versus Model 11).

Comparisons between models in Panel III also identify the form of interaction between U_EMP and age. The linear expression of age in this respect is significantly improved by the curvilinear expression of age (Model 8 versus Model 6), and the latter is further improved by the categorical expression of age (Model 11 versus Model 8).

Model 13 was estimated after looking at the results from Model 11. By observing that the parameter estimates for interaction effects of age and U_EMP do not significantly change at age 29 and over, the last six interaction terms are combined (see line 38 in Table 2.2). Model 13 provides a more parsimonious expression for the interaction effects than Model 11. The last model, Model 14, was tested, after including the interaction effects of age and U_EMP, to see whether the uniform and linear effects of age of employment are still more parsimonious than the categorical effects of age of employment. The test confirms that Model 13 is more parsimonious than Model 14.

In conclusion, Model 13 is the "best" model among the 14 models considered in Table 2.3.

Parameter estimates from selected models are presented in Table 2.4. The results indicate that (a) without the interaction effect of U_EMP and age, the linear effect of the age of employment, L_EMP, tends to be underestimated (compare Models 5, 8, and 13); and (b) even though Model 8 strongly improves the fit of Model 5, this model significantly distorts the pattern of age effects by using linear and quadratic terms for the interaction effect of U_EMP and age (compare Models 8 and 13).

Interpretation of Parameter Estimates

Parameters estimated from Model 13, which are presented in Table 2.4, are interpreted below for the effects of age and age of employment.

The Effects of Employment and Age of Employment

Here we have a pattern where the uniform effect, U_EMP, which applies to all different ages of employment, interacts with age in influencing the log-odds of getting married. The additional linear increase in the effect of employment as a function of age of employment (i.e., L_EMP) does not interact with age. Hence we first describe the "baseline" pattern of effects that apply to those who started employment under age 17. For those who started to work at age 17 or after, the pattern differs only by a constant amount that becomes the multiple of the coefficient for L_EMP, 0.053. The baseline pattern that characterizes the effect of ever had an employment, compared with never had an employment, on the log-odds of getting married needs to take into account the main effect of U_EMP and the interaction effects of U_EMP and age. The effects are summarized in Table 2.5.

The total effects in Table 2.5 show that the positive effects of ever had an employment on the log-odds of getting married monotonically decrease between ages 13 and 28. For example, the odds of getting married are 9.14 [= exp(2.213)] times higher during ages 15-16 for those who started their first employment under age 17 compared with those who never had an employment before; and the odds of getting married are 1.36 [= exp(0.310)] times higher during ages 27-28 for subjects in the former versus the latter employment category. The fact that all the employment effects are positive, regardless of age, supports Hypothesis 1. Rates of marriage are higher for those who started to work, thereby

Table 2.5
The "Baseline" Effects of Employment on the Log-Odds
of Getting Married

Age	Main Effect of U_EMP	Interaction with Age	Total Effect
13-14	0.501	1.869	2.370
15-16	0.501	1.712	2.213
17-18	0.501	1.003	1.504
19-20	0.501	0.470	0.971
21-22	0.501	0.000	0.501
23-24	0.501	-0.078	0.423
25-26	0.501	-0.148	0.353
27-28	0.501	-0.191	0.310
29-40	0.501	-0.012	0.489

satisfying the sequencing norm in which work precedes marriage. The fact that the effects of entering employment decrease as a function of age supports Hypothesis 2. Because the probability of violating the normative timing of marriage increases with age, the positive effect of having started to work on the rate of getting married decreases with age.

The effect of age of employment simply becomes additive to the effects presented in Table 2.5. The linear term for the age of employment assigns 0 for ages of employment under 17, 1 for ages 17-18, 2 for 19-20, 3 for 21-22, 4 for 23-24, and 5 for 25 and over, and the coefficient for this linear effect of age of employment is 0.053. Model 13 predicts that, compared with those who started to work before the age of 17, the odds of getting married are 1.05 [= exp(0.053)] time higher for those who started to work at ages 17-18 and 1.24 [= exp(4 × 0.053)] times higher for those who started to work at ages 23-24. The fact that the linear effect of the age of employment is significant and positive supports Hypothesis 3. As the age of employment increases, the effect of employment on the rate of getting married becomes larger, controlling for age.

Age Effects

Since the interaction effect of age and U_EMP is significant, the pattern of age effects differs depending on whether a subject has entered employment or not. Because U_EMP = 0 for "before employment," the interaction effects need to be taken into account only for the age effects "after employment." The age effects are summarized by

Table 2.6

Age Effects on the Log-Odds of Getting Married.

| | Before Employment | After Employment | |
Age	Total Effect	Interaction with U_EMP	Total Effect
13-14	-4.590	1.869	-2.721
15-16	-4.311	1.712	-2.599
17-18	-2.261	1.003	-1.258
19-20	-0.868	0.470	-0.398
21-22	[0.000]	[0.000]	[0.000]
23-24	0.199	-0.078	0.121
25-26	0.269	-0.148	0.121
27-28	0.221	-0.191	0.030
29-30	-0.088	-0.012	-0.100
31-32	-0.321	-0.012	-0.333
33-34	-0.576	-0.012	-0.588
35-36	-0.703	-0.012	-0.715
37-38	-0.869	-0.012	-0.881
38-40	-1.099	-0.012	-1.111

Table 2.6, where figures in the third column equal the sum of those in the first and second columns. Note that the columns are standardized with respect to the age category 21-22 and, therefore, the numbers are not directly comparable across columns.

The pattern of age effects in Table 2.6 indicates that the odds of getting married peak at ages 25-26 for those who have not entered employment and at ages 23-26 for those who have entered employment. Also, the increase in the log-odds of getting married from adolescence to young adulthood is much more rapid before employment compared with after employment. For example, for subjects who have not entered employment, the odds of getting married are 3.12 [= exp(.269 − [−.868])] times higher at ages 25-26 than at ages 19-20. After employment, the odds are 1.68 [= exp[.121 − (−.398)]] times higher for ages 25-26 versus ages 19-20.

Simultaneous Consideration of Age Effects and Age of Employment Effects

In order to assess the age effects and the age-of-employment effects simultaneously, the calculation of the following relative log-odds are useful: relative log-odds for age i and age of employment j = (main

Table 2.7

Relative Log-Odds of Getting Married as a Function of Experience of
Employment and Age of Employment
(contrast state: before employment, age 21-22)

			After Employment					
			Age of Employment					
	Before		*under 17*	*17-18*	*19-20*	*21-22*	*23-24*	*25+*
Age	*Employment*	*score*	*0*	*1*	*2*	*3*	*4*	*5*
13-14	-4.590		-2.220	—	—	—	—	—
15-16	-4.311		-2.098	—	—	—	—	—
17-18	-2.261		-0.758	-0.705	—	—	—	—
19-20	-0.868		0.103	0.156	0.209	—	—	—
21-22	[0.000]		0.501	0.553	0.606	0.659	—	—
23-24	0.199		0.622	0.675	0.727	0.780	0.832	—
25-26	0.269		0.622	0.675	0.727	0.780	0.832	0.885
27-28	0.221		0.530	0.583	0.635	0.688	0.741	0.793
29-30	-0.088		0.400	0.453	0.506	0.559	0.611	0.664
31-32	-0.321		0.167	0.220	0.273	0.325	0.378	0.430
33-34	-0.576		-0.087	-0.035	0.018	0.070	0.123	0.175
35-36	-0.703		-0.214	-0.162	-0.109	-0.057	-0.004	0.048
37-38	-0.869		-0.381	-0.328	-0.275	-0.223	-0.170	-0.118
39-40	-1.100		-0.611	-0.558	-0.506	-0.453	-0.401	-0.348

age effect for age i) + (interaction effect of age i and U_EMP) + (main effect of U_EMP) + (.053) × (score for age of employment for category j) × D, where $D = 1$ for after employment and $D = 0$ for before employment. The "score" for the age of employment is given in Table 2.7, which presents the relative log-odds of getting married, based on Model 13. Figure 2.3 depicts the relative log-odds for the following columns in Table 2.7: 1 (before employment), 2 (employment under 17), 4 (employment at 19-20), and 6 (employment at 23-24).

In addition to the characteristics described in the discussion of Tables 2.5 and 2.6, Table 2.7 shows that the odds of getting married among persons who have not entered employment are moderately high during ages 23-28. The odds of getting married for those who have entered employment are highest during ages 21-30, and moderately high at ages 19-20 and ages 31-32. Hence, for after employment compared with before employment, not only do moderately high odds of getting married start at younger ages, but high or moderately high odds of getting married last longer, especially when subjects enter employment later.

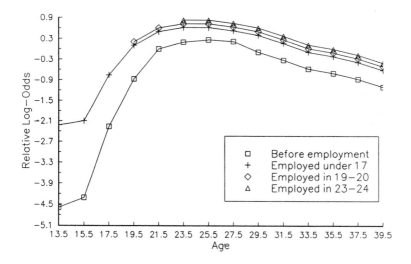

Figure 2.3. Getting Married

CONCLUDING REMARKS

Researchers who need to know more about the methodological foundation of the discrete-time logit model should refer to Allison (1982), Cox (1972), or Prentice and Gloeckler (1978). Textbooks such as those by Kalbfleisch and Prentice (1980), Cox and Oakes (1984), and McCullagh and Nelder (1989) include related material. For some additional sociological applications of the discrete-time logit models, see an analysis of divorce by Morgan and Rindfuss (1985), an analysis of migration by Massey (1987), and an analysis of birth timing by Teachman and Schollaert (1989).

PROBLEMS

(1) Identify which of the following *time-independent* explanatory variables are adequate to use and which are inadequate. Explain.

   (a) ever premaritally cohabited in predicting marriage

   (b) ever premaritally cohabited in predicting divorce

(c) marijuana use in high school in predicting dropping out of high school

(d) marijuana use in high school in predicting dropping out of college

(2) Table 2.8 presents aggregate data for the number of marriages and the number of persons at risk of marriage, cross-classified by age, age cohort, and a dichotomous distinction for before and after first employment. This data set is the same as that used in the analysis presented in this chapter, except that different ages of first employment are not distinguished. The variable labeled OBS indicates the number of observations for each row in Table 2.8, and the variable labeled EVT indicates the number of marriages. The difference between OBS and EVT represents the number of observations for which marriage did not occur. Using this data set, do the following:

(a) Test the proportional odds model that includes the effects of age, age cohort, and employment. Use two-year intervals in constructing a set of dummy variables for age. Treat the cohort effect categorically. Interpret the results.

(b) Test a parametric characterization for age effects by using a curvilinear function. Based on the likelihood-ratio chi-square test, confirm that this model fits the data worse than the model tested in (a).

(c) Test models that include alternative interaction effects of age and employment. Use (A) linear effect of age, (B) curvilinear effects of age, and (C) categorical effects of age. Based on the likelihood-ratio tests, confirm that Model C is the best-fitting model among the three.

(d) Describe the parameters estimated from Model C.

NOTES

1. How small should the conditional probabilities p be? Clogg and Eliason (1987) show that rate models can be used as an approximation for logit models if p is approximately 0.1 or smaller. Hence logit models can be used as an approximation for rate models under a similar condition. However, it may be too conservative to require the conditional probabilities to be consistently smaller than, say, 0.1 at all discrete time points and for all combinations of covariate values. In fact, we still get very similar results from continuous-time and discrete-time models for data sets where conditional probabilities exceed 0.1 at many discrete time points. However, we can reasonably expect that the approximation will not be adequate if the aggregate frequency data include a high proportion of situations where p becomes much larger than 0.1.

2. There are some differences among programs. For the analysis of discrete-time event history data, both SAS-LOGIST and BMDPLR are useful, while SPSSX-PROBIT has more limitations. The major difference between SAS-LOGIST and BMDPLR is that the latter, while providing certain conveniences, offers less flexibility in modeling.

Table 2.8
Data of Getting Married

CHT	AGE	EMP	OBS	EVT	CHT	AGE	EMP	OBS	EVT
0	13	0	5431	11	0	13	1	176	11
0	14	0	5325	1	0	14	1	260	3
0	15	0	5128	3	0	15	1	453	6
0	16	0	4822	9	0	16	1	750	23
0	17	0	4147	41	0	17	1	1393	75
0	18	0	3302	74	0	18	1	2123	223
0	19	0	2788	138	0	19	1	2341	351
0	20	0	2298	168	0	20	1	2341	458
0	21	0	1750	200	0	21	1	2264	475
0	22	0	1242	173	0	22	1	2097	469
0	23	0	834	113	0	23	1	1863	443
0	24	0	574	85	0	24	1	1566	375
0	25	0	376	68	0	25	1	1304	263
0	26	0	220	23	0	26	1	990	208
0	27	0	137	22	0	27	1	706	143
0	28	0	82	9	0	28	1	509	104
0	29	0	49	4	0	29	1	363	71
0	30	0	39	3	0	30	1	230	33
0	31	0	28	1	0	31	1	170	21
0	32	0	19	1	0	32	1	114	13
0	33	0	7	1	0	33	1	72	5
0	34	0	4	0	0	34	1	38	3
1	13	0	4258	8	1	13	1	267	6
1	14	0	4102	4	1	14	1	410	3
1	15	0	3860	5	1	15	1	645	8
1	16	0	3536	5	1	16	1	957	17
1	17	0	2988	19	1	17	1	1483	68
1	18	0	2414	50	1	18	1	1971	150
1	19	0	2033	94	1	19	1	2152	272
1	20	0	1749	117	1	20	1	2070	321
1	21	0	1403	149	1	21	1	1978	320
1	22	0	1082	158	1	22	1	1831	371
1	23	0	791	104	1	23	1	1593	316
1	24	0	583	77	1	24	1	1382	272
1	25	0	416	55	1	25	1	1199	250
1	26	0	303	40	1	26	1	1008	186
1	27	0	222	32	1	27	1	863	141
1	28	0	164	22	1	28	1	748	125
1	29	0	124	16	1	29	1	640	87
1	30	0	97	12	1	30	1	565	84
1	31	0	75	7	1	31	1	491	71
1	32	0	62	6	1	32	1	425	48
1	33	0	52	1	1	33	1	382	43

Continued

Table 2.8, Continued

CHT	AGE	EMP	OBS	EVT	CHT	AGE	EMP	OBS	EVT
1	34	0	46	0	1	34	1	343	28
1	35	0	39	1	1	35	1	322	27
1	36	0	36	1	1	36	1	271	32
1	37	0	29	2	1	37	1	213	12
1	38	0	25	1	1	38	1	180	14
1	39	0	22	3	1	39	1	143	12
1	40	0	16	1	1	40	1	119	9
2	13	0	4338	8	2	13	1	353	4
2	14	0	4167	2	2	14	1	513	1
2	15	0	3873	6	2	15	1	803	7
2	16	0	3437	9	2	16	1	1226	18
2	17	0	2908	18	2	17	1	1729	48
2	18	0	2404	36	2	18	1	2167	94
2	19	0	2005	63	2	19	1	2437	171
2	20	0	1680	88	2	20	1	2527	279
2	21	0	1385	114	2	21	1	2455	375
2	22	0	1125	147	2	22	1	2227	389
2	23	0	863	120	2	23	1	1953	342
2	24	0	645	88	2	24	1	1708	281
2	25	0	482	63	2	25	1	1502	279
2	26	0	347	47	2	26	1	1295	257
2	27	0	252	29	2	27	1	1085	191
2	28	0	194	21	2	28	1	924	156
2	29	0	155	16	2	29	1	786	133
2	30	0	127	10	2	30	1	666	87
2	31	0	102	7	2	31	1	594	77
2	32	0	85	4	2	32	1	527	47
2	33	0	76	3	2	33	1	485	43
2	34	0	73	1	2	34	1	443	36
2	35	0	67	1	2	35	1	411	23
2	36	0	63	1	2	36	1	392	25
2	37	0	60	2	2	37	1	368	26
2	38	0	56	1	2	38	1	345	16
2	39	0	50	1	2	39	1	334	17
2	40	0	48	2	2	40	1	318	14
3	13	0	3284	7	3	13	1	393	6
3	14	0	3073	1	3	14	1	592	1
3	15	0	2784	3	3	15	1	879	5
3	16	0	2473	9	3	16	1	1182	8
3	17	0	2108	14	3	17	1	1529	29
3	18	0	1734	23	3	18	1	1860	59
3	19	0	1421	31	3	19	1	2092	128
3	20	0	1147	29	3	20	1	2208	152
3	21	0	927	43	3	21	1	2247	235

Continued

Table 2.8, Continued

CHT	AGE	EMP	OBS	EVT	CHT	AGE	EMP	OBS	EVT
3	22	0	741	44	3	22	1	2155	240
3	23	0	598	37	3	23	1	2014	274
3	24	0	491	43	3	24	1	1810	273
3	25	0	397	45	3	25	1	1587	250
3	26	0	322	27	3	26	1	1367	216
3	27	0	279	26	3	27	1	1167	187
3	28	0	233	24	3	28	1	1000	150
3	29	0	193	13	3	29	1	866	122
3	30	0	168	14	3	30	1	756	113
3	31	0	146	8	3	31	1	651	82
3	32	0	134	5	3	32	1	572	77
3	33	0	124	8	3	33	1	501	53
3	34	0	112	14	3	34	1	453	47
3	35	0	94	6	3	35	1	409	46
3	36	0	85	2	3	36	1	366	35
3	37	0	81	5	3	37	1	333	30
3	38	0	74	4	3	38	1	304	24
3	39	0	70	4	3	39	1	281	15
3	40	0	65	3	3	40	1	267	13

For example, BMDPLR accounts for hierarchy among the main effects and interaction effects in the stepwise regression, and can automatically generate the design matrix for categorical variables and their interactions with other variables. SAS-LOGIST has none of these features. However, BMDPLR cannot employ both categorical and linear versions of the same variable simultaneously in the model. Therefore, when the main effects of a variable are expressed categorically, the variable must also be expressed categorically in defining its interactions with other variables. SAS-LOGIST, on the other hand, does not have such restrictions.

3

Discrete-Time Logit Models, II: The Analysis of Two-Way Transitions

METHODS AND MODELS

This chapter extends logit models for discrete-time event history data to analyze transitions between two states. The analysis requires that transitions in each direction are repeatable events. The logit models of two-way transitions can be used for two different reasons: (a) to approximate a pair of continuous-time processes that characterize transitions between two states, and (b) to model the sequence of binary responses from panel data. Although both types of applications are described, the example presented in this chapter illustrates the latter use.

The use of discrete-time logit models for the analysis of two-way transitions is beneficial, compared with logit models that analyze each transition separately, when a kind of symmetry in the effects of covariates exists for at least some covariates. This issue is discussed below.

Models that are similar to those described in this chapter are discussed in the work of Heckman (1981) and Yamaguchi (1990b). They are also related to models of binary time series (e.g., Cox, 1970, chap. 5; Liang & Zeger, 1989).

Modeling Repeatable Events

A *repeatable event* is an event that occurs more than once for at least some subjects in the sample. The distinction between repeatable and nonrepeatable events is in part operationally defined because the first occurrence of a repeatable event can be analyzed as a nonrepeatable event. Multiple duration intervals each of which corresponds to a distinct (possible) occurrence of the repeatable event are referred to as *spells*. For example, in the analysis of divorce, we may have multiple marriage spells for the same subject.

The analysis of repeatable events requires a stronger assumption than the analysis of nonrepeatable events. It is usually assumed that, controlling for covariates, multiple spells for each subject are *conditionally independent*. In other words, for a repeatable event we usually assume a *modulated renewal process*, with a common baseline hazard function among spells (Kalbfleisch & Prentice, 1980). A renewal process is a stochastic process with spells that are identically and independently distributed (Cox & Lewis, 1966). The modulated renewal process generalizes the renewal process by allowing covariates to modulate interdependence among spells.[1] Specifically, covariates can take into account characteristics of preceding event histories.

Some repeatable events, however, may not be characterized adequately by a modulated renewal process, no matter what covariates are used to reflect interdependence among multiple spells. For example, becoming divorced and getting remarried may both be regarded as repeatable events for which a group of marriage spells and a group of divorce spells can each be modeled by a modulated renewal process. However, it seems wrong to group the first marriage and remarriages together as occurrences of a repeatable event, because entry into the risk period is defined quite differently for the two. While the risk period of a remarriage starts with the occurrence of a divorce, the risk period of the first marriage starts at a certain age. The major time dimension for the first marriage is age, and the major time dimension for remarriages is the duration of divorce, although age may become an important time-dependent covariate for the occurrence of a remarriage. Hence we should not group them together, and the occurrence of the first marriage should be analyzed separately as a nonrepeatable event.

Generally, the first entry into a particular state can be quite different in nature from reentries. Therefore, it may be adequate to apply a modulated renewal process model only to reentries. Since reentries may not occur for every subject in the sample, findings are usually limited with respect to generalizability.

Two Different Uses of the Logit Model
for the Analysis of Two-Way Transitions

The logit model for the analysis of two-way transitions may be employed for two reasons. One reason to use it is as an approximation for a pair of continuous-time processes that characterize transitions between two states. Since the logit model must approximate a continuous-time

Table 3.1

The Frequency Distribution for Dependent States Without Censored
Observations

| | Panel I: Nonrepeatable Event, One-Way Transition | | | | | Panel II: Repeatable Events, Two-Way Transition | | | | |
	$t = 1$	$t = 2$	$t = 3$	$t = 4$	$t = 5$	$t = 1$	$t = 2$	$t = 3$	$t = 4$	$t = 5$
$Y = 1$	$f1$	$f2$	$f3$	$f4$	$f5$	$f1$	$f2$	$f3$	$f4$	$f5$
$Y = 0$	$F1$	$F2$	$F3$	$F4$	$F5$	$g1$	$g2$	$g3$	$g4$	$g5$
Total	$F0$	$F1$	$F2$	$F3$	$F4$	$F0$	$F0$	$F0$	$F0$	$F0$
	where $Fi = F(i - 1) - fi$, for $i = 1, \ldots, 5$					where $Fi = fi + gi$ for $i = 1, \ldots, 5$				

model adequately for each direction of transition, both conditional probabilities (of transition from state 0 to state 1, given state 0, and transition from state 1 to state 0, given state 1) have to be sufficiently small.

The second reason for the use of the logit model is based on a different assumption. First, look at Table 3.1, where the frequency distribution of a nonrepeatable one-way transition is compared with that of a repeatable two-way transition for cases with no censored observations.

For the analysis of a nonrepeatable event, subjects who have the event are removed from the risk set. Therefore, the frequency in the second row of Table 3.1 (where $Y = 0$) determines the number of sample subjects who are at risk at the next time point. Accordingly, the total frequency decreases with time. On the other hand, for the analysis of repeatable two-way transitions, nobody leaves the risk set because the occurrence of a transition puts the subject at risk for the reverse transition. Accordingly, the total frequency remains the same regardless of time.

The data presented in Panel II in Table 3.1 can be thought of as frequency distributions for five distinct variables (i.e., Y_i, $i = 1, \ldots, 5$) for $F0$ subjects. It follows from this view that Panel II of Table 3.1 is not a contingency table.

Under a certain assumption, however, we may take an alternative view that the data represent a contingency table for a cross-classification of a single variable, Y, with time among $5 \times F0$ subjects. This alternative view is not correct for all cases, but becomes acceptable under the assumption that the pattern of interdependence among multiple observations for each subject is correctly specified in the model. Therefore, controlling for factors included in the model, the observations at different time points become conditionally independent.

The view that assumes that observations across time points are conditionally independent is implicitly employed by many researchers who base their analyses on a pooled sample from multiples waves of a panel survey. This view, however, will never be valid if Panel II in Table 3.1 is generated from a cross-sectional survey by a retrospective recall of states. While the conditional independence of multiple-wave observations is a very strong assumption,[2] it may be acceptable for certain variables. The assumption permits applications of the logit model for the panel data analysis of two-way transitions regardless of the size of conditional probabilities for having each direction of transition.

Two-Way Transition Models

Suppose $\{Y_t\}$ is a process that takes either -1 or 1 at each discrete time t. Let S_0 denote the state for which $Y_t = -1$, and let S_1 denote the state for which $Y_t = 1$. Finally, let P_t denote the probability $P(Y_t = 1)$. Then, suppose we have a logit model such that

$$\ln [P_t / (1 - P_t)] = b_0 + b_1 Y_{t-1} + b_2 X_t + b_3 Z_t + b_4 Y_{t-1} Z_t \qquad (3.1)$$

where X_t is a covariate for which the interaction with Y_{t-1} is not hypothesized in the model, and Z_t is a covariate for which the interaction with Y_{t-1} is hypothesized in the model. Then it can be easily shown (Yamaguchi, 1990b) that

b_2 represents the effect of X_t on the transition from S_0 to S_1. (3.2)
$-b_2$ represents the effect of X_t on the transition from S_1 to S_0.
b_3-b_4 represents the effect of Z_t on the transition from S_0 to S_1.
$-(b_3+b_4)$ represents the effect of Z_t on the transition from S_1 to S_0.

The effect of X_t or Z_t implies a change in the *log-odds* of having the transition here. Hence the logit model given in Formula 3.1 is a model of odds of two-way transitions. Note that the effect of Z_t on the transition from S_0 (at time $t-1$) to S_1 (at time t) is given as the coefficient of Z_t when $Y_{t-1} = -1$ and is equal to $(b_3 - b_4)$. The effect of Z_t on the reverse transition becomes clear when we let $Q_t = P(Y_t = -1)$, and rewrite Formula 3.1 as follows:

$$\ln [Q_t / (1 - Q_t)] = \ln [(1 - P_t) / P_t] \\ = -b_0 - b_1 Y_{t-1} - b_2 X_t - b_3 Z_t - b_4 Y_{t-1} Z_t \qquad (3.3)$$

The effect of Z_t on the transition from S_1 at time $t - 1$ to S_0 at time t is given as the coefficient of Z_t in Formula 3.3 when $Y_{t - 1} = 1$ and is equal to $-(b_3 + b_4)$.

Although the model described in Formula 3.1 has only two covariates, X and Z can be replaced by sets of covariates X and Z. Only covariates in the covariate-vector Z have an interaction effect with $Y_{t - 1}$ such that

$$\ln [P_t / (1 - P_t)] = b_0 + b_1 Y_{t-1} + b'_2 X_t + b'_3 Z_t + b'_4 Z_t Y_{t-1} \qquad (3.4)$$

Then, the effects of X_t on the log-odds of transition from S_0 to S_1 and from S_1 to S_0 can be given by vectors b_2 and $-b_2$, respectively, and those of Z_t can be given by vectors $b_3 - b_4$ and $-(b_3 + b_4)$, respectively.

We can thus simultaneously model transitions between two states. If necessary, we can obtain separate estimates for the effect of each covariate on each transition by including interactions between $Y_{t - 1}$ and covariates in the model. Whether or not a given covariate interacts significantly with $Y_{t - 1}$ is a matter that should be empirically determined. As the number of covariates that have no interaction effects with $Y_{t - 1}$ becomes larger, the modeling of two-way transitions becomes more parsimonious compared with a separate modeling of each of the two transitions. A separate modeling always uses two parameters for a given covariate: one parameter for one transition and the other parameter for the reverse transition. On the other hand, for a given covariate, only one parameter is needed to characterize its effects on both ways of transition when the interaction of the covariate with $Y_{t - 1}$ is absent.

Modeling Duration Dependence

The major time dimension in the analysis of two-way transitions as repeatable events is the duration of time since the last transition. Some alternative specifications for modeling duration dependence are described below.

Linear Duration Effect

Suppose that covariate $LD_{t - 1}$ represents the linear duration of the state observed at time $t - 1$, that is, the length of sequences without any transition up to time $t - 1$. Then, from Formulas 3.1 and 3.2, we obtain the duration effect at S_0 by $(b_2 - b_3)$ and that at S_1 by $-(b_2 + b_3)$ when we include both the LD_{t-1} and its interaction with Y_{t-1}—that is, $b_2 LD_{t-1} + b_3 LD_{t-1} Y_{t-1}$—in the model. Since duration effects are usually negative—that is, $(b_2 - b_3) < 0$ and $-(b_2 + b_3) < 0$—b_3 is usually positive and larger than $|b_2|$. Hence the interaction term $LD_{t-1} Y_{t-1}$ normally needs to be included in the model.

Suppose we wish to test a model where the linear duration effect of being in one state is hypothesized to be *identical in amount* to the linear duration effect of being in the other state of the dependent process. Such a model is given by including *only the interaction of LD_{t-1} with Y_{t-1}* in the model, that is, $b_3 LD_{t-1} Y_{t-1}$. Estimates of the linear duration effect for both states S_0 and S_1 are then given by $-b_3$.

Categorical Duration Effect

The categorical expression for the duration effect can be simply modeled by defining a set of dummy duration variables such that

$D_1 = 1$ if and only if $Y_{t-1} \neq Y_{t-2}$,   and becomes 0 otherwise;

$D_2 = 1$ if and only if $Y_{t-1} = Y_{t-2} \neq Y_{t-3}$ and becomes 0 otherwise;

$D_3 = 1$ if and only if $Y_{t-1} = Y_{t-2} = Y_{t-3} \neq Y_{t-4}$,
     and becomes 0 otherwise;

$D_{s-1} = 1$ if and only if $Y_{t-1} = \ldots = Y_{t-s+1} \neq Y_{t-s}$,
     and becomes 0 otherwise;

$D_s = 1$ if and only if $Y_{t-1} = \ldots = Y_{t-s+1} = Y_{t-s}$,
     and becomes 0 otherwise.

$$(3.5)$$

Each variable D_i, $i = 1, \ldots, s - 1$, represents the duration of i time points and variable D_s represents the duration of s time points *and over*. Since the amount of duration is more than or equal to one, one of the dummy variables needs to be omitted. It is useful to specify the state of one duration—that is, $Y_{t-1} \neq Y_{t-2}$—as the baseline state and thereby omit D_1 from the model. Then, similar to the case described above, if we include

$$b_2 D_2 + b_3 D_3 + \ldots + b_s D_s + [c_2 D_2 + c_3 D_3 + \ldots + c_s D_s] Y_{t-1} \quad (3.6)$$

in the model, the duration effects of state S_0 are characterized by a set of coefficients $(b_2 - c_2)$, $(b_3 - c_3)$, $\ldots$, $(b_s - c_s)$, and those at state S_1

are characterized by $-(b_2 + c_2)$, $-(b_3 + c_3)$, . . . , $-(b_s + c_s)$, respectively, for the duration of 2, 3, . . . , $s - 1$, and s-and-more time points compared with the duration of one time point.

Duration Dependence with a Truncation

In the use of a set of dummy duration variables in Formula 3.6, it is implicitly assumed that the duration effect of $s + 1$ or more time points is the same in amount as the duration effect of s time points. Special cases of duration effects, which we refer to as *truncated duration dependence*, explicitly assume this characteristic for a small number of s.

Suppose that $s = 1$. It follows that we do not include any of the dummy duration variables, $D_2, D_3, . . . , D_s$ in the model, and we obtain a *Markov process model*. The Markov process model with discrete-time unit assumes that none of the previous states of Y_s for $s < t$, other than the immediately preceding state—that is, Y_{t-1}—influence the outcome at time t.

A simple generalization of the Markovian model is obtained when $s = 2$. The model has only one dummy duration variable D_2 that satisfies $D_2 = 0$ if $Y_{t-1} \neq Y_{t-2}$ and $D_2 = 1$ if $Y_{t-1} = Y_{t-2}$. This model assumes that none of the previous states of Y_s for $s < t$, other than the two immediately preceding states—Y_{t-1} and Y_{t-2}—influences the outcome at time t.

It turns out that the use of D_2 as the only covariate for duration effects is equivalent to the use of Y_{t-2} as a covariate, provided that the interaction of D_2 or Y_{t-2} with Y_{t-1} is also introduced in the respective model. Generally, given two models such that

$$\ln [P_t /(1 - P_t)] = b_0 + b_1 Y_{t-1} + b_2 D_2 + b_3 Y_{t-1} D_2 \ldots \qquad (3.7a)$$

$$\ln [P_t /(1 - P_t)] = c_0 + c_1 Y_{t-1} + c_2 Y_{t-2} + c_3 Y_{t-1} Y_{t-2} \ldots \qquad (3.7b)$$

it can be shown easily that $b_0 = c_0 - c_3$; $b_1 = c_1 - c_2$; $b_2 = 2c_3$; and $b_3 = 2c_2$. It follows that the duration effects at states S_0 and S_1 are respectively given by the following:

$$b_2 - b_3 = 2(-c_2 + c_3) \qquad (3.8a)$$

$$-(b_2 + b_3) = -2(c_2 + c_3) \qquad (3.8b)$$

In particular, for the model that hypothesizes that the duration effect at S_0 is equal in amount to the duration effect at S_1, the coefficient is given by $-b_3 = -2c_2$. Hence the model that introduces Y_{t-2} *without including its interaction with* Y_{t-1}, represents a model in which (a) the duration effects characterized by D_2 are equal in size for the two states, and (b) the amount of the duration effects becomes minus twice the coefficient of Y_{t-2}. If the duration effects of the two states are different, however, then the interaction between Y_{t-1} and Y_{t-2} should be significant, and the effects are given by Formulas 3.8a and 3.8b.

The extension of models described above for $s > 2$ assumes that for a given particular time s that is prior to the current time t by a fixed amount, the effect of duration for s units of time and longer becomes uniform. Therefore, knowledge of states prior to time $t - s$ is uninformative in predicting the state at time t. The models of such truncated duration dependence become useful, if they are appropriate empirically, for modeling psychological/attitudinal dependent variables, which are discussed below.

Additional Dimensions of Time

In addition to duration effects, repeatable events often depend on other time dimensions. These dimensions need to be taken into account as time-dependent covariates. For example, in the analysis of panel data, period effects, which reflect different waves of the panel, normally exist. In the analysis of remarriages, age will be relevant. And in the analysis of interfirm job separations for which duration of work with the same employer is the major time dimension, cumulative length of work experience may be important.

Models for Attitudinal or Social Psychological Dependent Variables

Event history analysis is most appropriate for events that have a clearly defined risk period. Transitions between different demographic statuses, such as marital and employment statuses, are such examples. Variables that indicate the occurrences of certain behaviors, such as the use of illicit drugs, can be used to define the dependent variable so long as accurate measurements for the occurrences of the behaviors can be assumed.

On the other hand, psychological or attitudinal variables are much more limited in defining dependent states and events. First, we do not know exactly when the event (i.e., a change in the state) occurs. But we may define an event as a change in the state of a variable over one unit of time for given equally spaced discrete-time measurements of the variable. Similarly, the duration of a particular psychological/attitudinal state can be defined as the length of the sequence of the same state for given discrete-time measurements. However, we usually do not know when the risk for having a change in attitude or in psychological state started. In other words, we always have a problem of left truncation for this type of duration variable.

However, under certain situations—namely, situations where models with truncated duration dependence can be adequately applied—we are able to use psychological/attitudinal variables to define dependent states and events. For example, suppose that the process is Markovian—that is, a process where the state of the dependent variable at time t depends only on its immediately preceding state at $t - 1$ and exogenous covariates. If this condition holds true, then knowledge of the state at t_0 permits us to predict the states of the dependent variable at $t_0 + 1$ and afterward, without knowing states of the variable prior to time t_0.

The Markovian assumption, however, is very strong and may not be satisfied empirically. But we can generalize the model by allowing a less stringent truncated dependence on past states. Indeed, it is often observed for psychological/attitudinal variables that the effects of previous states of the dependent variable, such as those observed at times $t - 1$, $t - 2$, $t - 3$, and so on, on the current state, that is, the state at time t, attenuate rather rapidly as time goes back.[3] Generally, if the current state at time t depends only on the states at time $t - 1$, $t - 2$, . . . , $t - s$, then the knowledge of conditions at particular times t_0, $t_0 + 1$, . . . , $t_0 + s - 1$ allows us to model the process at time $t_0 + s$ and afterward, without introducing bias in parameter estimates due to the left truncation of observation at time t_0. In this chapter, I apply models that reflect such a truncated duration dependence for the analysis of personal efficacy based on panel survey data.

APPLICATION: A DYNAMIC ANALYSIS
OF PERSONAL EFFICACY

Data and Covariates

The data set used here is from the Panel Study of Income Dynamics (PSID), 1968-1972 (Duncan & Morgan, 1985; Morgan, Dickinson, Dickinson, Benus, & Duncan, 1974). The first five waves of this survey collected items pertaining to personal efficacy, and an index of personal efficacy is available for the analysis. For the first four waves, the original investigators created an index based on seven items. For the fifth wave, they dropped one of the seven items from the survey and, therefore, created an index based on six items. In order to eliminate inconsistency in measurement, I reconstructed the index for the first four waves by omitting the component item that was dropped in the fifth wave. The original index thus reformulated takes integer values from 0 to 6 as the sum of six dichotomous items. I further dichotomized the index by collapsing values 0 to 3 for the low level of personal efficacy, and values 4 to 6 for the high level.

The PSID does not use individuals as the sampling unit, but instead uses households. The survey collects various data from individual household heads and their spouses. A problem here is that, although the personal efficacy measure is available for the household head from each sample household, the head may change over time. The survey, however, has information about whether the household head for each year is the same as that of the previous year. I restricted the analysis to households that were consistently headed by the same male from 1968 to 1972. It follows that the analysis presented below has a limitation regarding the generalizability of findings because those who remain as the head for five years may not be a representative sample of male household heads in the population.

Five variables are taken into account as covariates. The first two are the time-lagged variables of personal efficacy measured at times $t - 1$ and $t - 2$ in predicting the state of personal efficacy at time t. The use of these variables is based on the assumption that personal efficacy at time t does not depend on its state at time s, where $s < t - 2$, once the states at times $t - 1$ and $t - 2$ are taken into account—which approximately holds true empirically.[4] Because two time-lagged variables are used, the data for the first two years (1968 and 1969) are

Table 3.2

Data of Personal Efficacy: Men Who Are Consistently Household
Heads During 1968-1972 (Panel Study of Income Dynamics)

		Covariates			Frequency	
Dep(t - 1)	Dep(t - 2)	Time	Divorce	Unemployment	Dep(t) = 0	Dep(t) = 1
0	0	1	0	0	3201	822
0	0	1	0	1	499	81
0	0	1	1	0	56	5
0	0	1	1	1	0	2
0	0	2	0	0	3218	719
0	0	2	0	1	524	122
0	0	2	1	0	35	7
0	0	2	1	1	7	0
0	0	3	0	0	3176	676
0	0	3	0	1	682	119
0	0	3	1	0	47	6
0	0	3	1	1	24	0
0	1	1	0	0	763	660
0	1	1	0	1	103	57
0	1	1	1	0	7	9
0	1	1	1	1	3	7
0	1	2	0	0	776	495
0	1	2	0	1	167	66
0	1	2	1	0	3	0
0	1	2	1	1	0	0
0	1	3	0	0	819	624
0	1	3	0	1	113	17
0	1	3	1	0	17	2
0	0	3	1	1	0	0
1	0	1	0	0	746	949
1	0	1	0	1	112	85
1	0	1	1	0	14	3
1	0	1	1	1	2	0
1	0	2	0	0	680	647
1	0	2	0	1	155	119
1	0	2	1	0	20	13
1	0	2	1	1	9	0
1	0	3	0	0	553	656
1	0	3	0	1	105	77
1	0	3	1	0	4	13
1	0	3	1	1	1	0
1	1	1	0	0	544	1723
1-	1	1	0	1	79	195
1	1	1	1	0	10	16
1	1	1	1	1	0	5
1	1	2	0	0	667	1934

Continued

Table 3.2, Continued

Dep(t - 1)	Dep(t - 2)	Covariates Time	Divorce	Unemployment	Frequency Dep(t) = 0	Dep(t) = 1
1	1	2	0	1	93	243
1	1	2	1	0	18	10
1	1	2	1	1	6	5
1	1	3	0	0	641	1987
1	1	3	0	1	94	224
1	1	3	1	0	8	16
1	1	3	1	1	1	0

used only for the construction of covariates. The dependent variable is thus measured only for the last three waves of the survey.

The third covariate included in the model is the categorical variable for the year of the survey. Since the dependent variable is measured at three different years (1970-1972), this categorical variable introduces a set of two parameters. The categorical variable is used because of the expected nonlinearity in period effects.

The fourth and fifth variables are included in order to test substantive hypotheses regarding the effects of stressful life events on personal efficacy. One variable reflects the effect of having a divorce between times $t - 1$ and t on the level of personal efficacy at time t. The variable takes a value of 1 if the subject experienced a divorce, and takes the value 0 otherwise. The other variable reflects the effect of unemployment between times $t - 1$ and t on the level of personal efficacy at time t. This variable takes a value of 1 when the subject experiences unemployment, and takes the value 0 otherwise. Both variables are time-dependent covariates of personal efficacy.

Table 3.2 presents the cross-classified frequency data for the dependent variable and its covariates. The data are used for the following analysis.

Substantive Hypotheses

Seven substantive hypotheses are tested with this data set. Two hypotheses pertain to the Markovian effect (i.e., the effect of personal efficacy at time $t - 1$) and the truncated duration effect (i.e., the effect of personal efficacy at time $t - 2$). The remaining five hypotheses pertain to the effects of divorce and unemployment on personal efficacy. No specific hypotheses are made for period effects.

- *Hypothesis 1:* There will be a strong effect of personal efficacy at time $t - 1$ on the level of personal efficacy at time t.
- *Hypothesis 2:* There will be a duration effect, measured as the effect of personal efficacy at time $t - 2$, on the level of personal efficacy at time t.
- *Hypothesis 3:* If the subject experienced a divorce in the preceding year, the rate of change from high to low personal efficacy will increase.
- *Hypothesis 4:* If the subject experienced a divorce in the preceding year, the rate of change from low to high personal efficacy will decrease.
- *Hypothesis 5:* If the subject experienced unemployment in the preceding year, the rate of change from high to low personal efficacy will increase.
- *Hypothesis 6:* If the subject experienced unemployment in the preceding year, the rate of change from low to high personal efficacy will decrease.
- *Hypothesis 7:* Assuming that the experience of divorce is more stressful than the experience of unemployment, the effects described in Hypotheses 3 and 4 will be respectively stronger than the effects described in Hypotheses 5 and 6.

Programming of Models

As in the case of models presented in Chapter 2, logistic regression is used to estimate parameters. In this chapter, we use BMDPLR because we consistently assume categorical effect of time and will be interested in various levels of higher-order interactions. Although BMDPLR does not directly provide the likelihood-ratio chi-square L^2, it can be calculated from the value of the log-likelihood that it provides. The program also provides likelihood-ratio chi-square for goodness-of-fit tests G^2 for aggregate input data. (See Chapter 2 for a review of L^2 and G^2.)

Table 3.3 provides an example of a program for a stepwise logistic regression that may be applied to the data. The program presented in Table 3.3 uses SAS to call the BMDPLR program because the SAS program generally permits more flexible data transformations than the BMDP program.

The first three lines of Table 3.3 create an SAS data file. Seven variables (DEP, DEP1, DEP2, TIME, DIV, UEMP, FREQ) are read from a non-SAS file called DKDATA. The variable DEP represents the 0-1 dichotomous variable for the dependent states at time t. Variables DEP1 and DEP2 are time-lagged values of DEP at times $t - 1$

Table 3.3

A Program for Logit Models for Discrete-Time Event History Analysis
of Two-Way Transitions

	Line[a]
DATA FRQDT;	1
INFILE DKDATA;	2
INPUT DEP 1 DEP1 2 DEP2 3 TIME 4 DIV 5 UEMP 6 FREQ 7-10;	3
PROC BMDP PROG=BMDPLR DATA=FRQDT;	4
PARMCARDS;	5
/INPUT UNIT=3. CODE='FRQDT'.	6
/REGR	7
DEPEND = DEP.	8
COUNT = FREQ.	9
CATEG = DEP1, DEP2, TIME, DIV, UEMP.	10
MODEL = DEP1*DEP2*TIME*UEMP, DEP1*DEP2*DIV, DEP1*TIME*DIV,11	
DEP1*DIV*UEMP, DEP2*TIME*DIV, DEP2*DIV*UEMP.	
RULE = MULT.	12
START = OUT, OUT, OUT, OUT, OUT, OUT.	13
MOVE = 4, 4, 4, 4, 4, 4.	14
ENTER = .010, .010.	15
REMOVE = .010, .010.	16
/END	17
/FINISH	18
;	19

a. Line numbers do not appear in the program.

and $t - 2$, respectively. TIME is the year of survey and takes 1, 2 and 3, respectively, for years 1970, 1971, and 1972. DIV and UEMP are time-varying dummy variables for the experience of divorce and unemployment during the period $(t - 1, t)$, as described before. The frequencies of their cross-classifications are given in Table 3.2.

Line 4, PROC BMDP, calls the logistic regression program BMDPLR from BMDP. The next line, PARMCARDS, indicates the beginning of the BMDP program. Line 6, INPUT, is special for the use of a BMDP program through SAS. Unit = 3 should be specified here, and CODE should correspond to the SAS name of the input data file.

Lines 8-17 specify the details of the stepwise logistic regression. Line 8 specifies the dependent variable DEP. Line 9, COUNT = FREQ, indicates that aggregate frequency data are used for input and the variable FREQ represents the frequency for each record.

Table 3.4

Design Matrix

	Value	Design Variables	
		(1)	*(2)*
DEP1	0	-1	
	1	1	
DEP2	0	-1	
	1	1	
TIME	1	-1	-1
	2	1	0
	3	0	1
DIV	0	-1	
	1	1	
UEMP	0	-1	
	1	1	

Line 10 specifies that the listed covariates are categorical. By default, line 10 also leads to the use of a design matrix that contrasts each category of a covariate with its first category, which is coded as −1. Table 3.4 presents the design matrix created by default for DEP1, DEP2, TIME, DIV, and UEMP. Researchers who wish to use conventional dummy variable expressions (i.e., 1 versus 0) should specify DVAR = PART.

The MODEL statement in line 11 specifies the highest levels of interactions that should be considered in the stepwise logistic regression. If researchers wish to consider all possible higher-order interactions for categorical covariates, they can simply specify the product of all covariates in the model statement. For example, the highest level of interactions among the five categorical covariates specified in line 10 becomes MODEL = DEP1*DEP2*TIME*DIV*UEMP. However, results from this specification are reliable only if the observed cross-classified data have no zero frequencies in any cell. The imposition of marginal frequencies that have zero observations leads to a warning message that "ABOVE ITEM DID NOT PASS THE TOLERANCE TEST" for the estimates of some parameters in the output.

In the present application, the cross-classified data have some zero-frequency cells (see Table 3.2). Therefore, the use of the highest level of interaction, or the use of TIME*DIV*UEMP, DEP1*DEP2*DIV*UEMP, or DEP1*DEP2*TIME*DIV as covariates, leads to the imposition of zero marginal frequencies. This can be confirmed by constructing respective marginal frequency tables from Table 3.2. (Do not forget to cross-classify each of them with DEP, too.) The particular specification of the model made in line 11 avoids the use of each of these higher-order interactions, while considering all interactions of lower levels. Hence, except for the avoidance of the imposition of zero marginal frequencies, models considered here do not have any other restrictions for testing the interaction effects of covariates.

The next five lines, 12 through 16, together specify criteria for entry and removal of factors from the model. The START statement in line 13 specifies whether each factor specified in the MODEL statement, including their lower-order effects, should be initially in or out of the model. The default specification is IN. Here OUT is specified in order to obtain the value of the log-likelihood for the constant probability model as well as the log-likelihood for each model tested in sequence in the stepwise regression. Line 14 specifies the number of times that factors can be entered in or removed from the model.

It is important to specify RULE = MULT (line 12) when the factors are OUT initially. The default rule is SING. Both rules, MULT and SING, take into account the hierarchy among factors, regarding levels of interactions, when factors are considered for entry or removal. (See Chapter 4 for more about the hierarchy among models.) But while rule SING considers only one factor at a time for entry into or removal from the model in each step, rule MULT permits multiple factors for entry into and removal from the model in each step. It follows that if SING is specified when the factors are initially OUT, a lower-level factor that is insignificant prevents the entry of all higher-order interactions that include this factor, no matter how strongly significant their effects are. Hence MULT must be specified when factors are initially OUT.

On the other hand, the use of the rule MULT can cause a set of factors to circulate in and out of the model repeatedly. The final model, then, may depend on the initial conditions (i.e., IN or OUT) and the number of times these factors are allowed to be entered into or removed from the model. Hence researchers should be careful in identifying the best-fitting model from the stepwise procedure because the last model is not necessarily the best-fitting model.

Lines 15 and 16 specify the P levels for entry and removal, respectively. Since the sample size is large, a strong criterion of a 1% significance level is employed for both entry and removal.

Description of Three Models

Table 3.5 presents the results from selected models. Model 1 includes only the Markovian effect, that is, the effect of DEP1 (the time-lagged value of DEP at time $t - 1$). This model becomes the constant hazard-rate model and serves as the baseline for comparison with other models. Note that if no covariates were included, the model would represent a constant probability of responses that is independently applied over time. In the analysis of two-way transitions, however, the constant hazard-rate model refers to transition rates (or transition odds) between two states that are both constant. Model 1 characterizes the two constant transition odds with two coefficients, one for DEP1 and the other for the intercept. The coefficient for DEP1 affects the absolute size of the two constant transition odds. A larger coefficient—that is, a larger Markovian effect—is associated with smaller transition odds for both the transition from state 0 to state 1 and that from state 1 to state 0. The intercept parameter determines the *relative* odds of transition between the two states. For Model 1, the intercept parameter is negative and means that the odds are smaller for the transition from state 0 (low personal efficacy) to state 1 (high personal efficacy), compared with the odds of the reverse transition.

Model 2 is the most parsimoniously fitting model among *proportional odds models* (models that assume the absence of interaction effects between any exogenous covariate and each of the two dimensions of time, i.e., TIME and DEP2). The model also assumes no interaction effects of TIME and DEP2. The proportional odds models, however, permit the effects of exogenous covariates (i.e., DIV and UEMP) and the effects of the two time dimensions (i.e., TIME and DEP2) to depend on the direction of transition—that is, their interaction effects with DEP1 are allowed. In other words, Model 2 is identified as the most parsimoniously fitting model at a given 1% criterion for entry and removal of factors when we specify the following model statement:

MODEL = DEP1*DIV*UEMP, DEP1*DEP2, DEP1*TIME.

On the other hand, Model 3 in Table 3.5 is the most parsimoniously fitting model identified by the stepwise logistic regression described in Table 3.3. Hence this is the most parsimoniously fitting model

Table 3.5
Results from Selected Models Applied to the Data of Table 3.1

Covariates		Model 1	Model 2	Model 3
(1)	DEP1	0.906***	0.745***	0.759***
(2)	DEP2	—	0.546***	0.488***
(3)	DEP2*DEP1	—	-0.037**	-0.035**
(4)	TIME:(1) 1971	—	-0.077***	-0.210*
	(2) 1972	—	-0.010	0.034
(5)	TIME*DEP1:(1)	—	—	-0.084
	(2)	—	—	0.398***
(6)	TIME*DEP2:(1)	—	—	-0.181
	(2)	—	—	-0.233*
(7)	TIME*DEP1*DEP2:(1)	—	—	0.072***
	(2)	—	—	-0.038*
(8)	UEMP	—	-0.135***	-0.133***
(9)	DIV	—	-0.320***	-0.358***
(10)	DIV*DEP1	—	—	0.012
(11)	DIV*DEP2	—	—	-0.056
(12)	DIV*TIME: (1)	—	—	-0.119
	(2)	—	—	0.033
(13)	DIV*DEP1*TIME:(1)	—	—	-0.082
	(2)	—	—	0.377***
(14)	DIV*DEP2*TIME:(1)	—	—	-0.163
	(2)	—	—	-0.256*
(15)	Constant	-0.235***	-0.585***	-0.623***
	G^2	1958.336***	113.044***	55.477***
	df	44	38	24
	(G^2: each model)/(G^2: Model 1)		.058	.028
	L^2 (against Model 1)	0.00	1845.292***	1902.859***
	df	0	6	20

$^{*}p < .050;\ ^{**}p < .010;\ ^{***}p < .001$

among models that do not impose any zero marginal frequencies. In terms of goodness-of-fit chi-square, however, neither Model 2 nor Model 3 fits the data very well (the G^2 values of both are still significant at the .001% level). In fact, the most general model that includes all factors except those that impose zero marginal frequencies does not fit the data at an adequate level (results not represented). However, compared with the constant transition rate model (Model 1), Model 2 explains about 94% [= 1 − 113.04/1958.34] of the chi-square and Model 3 explains about 97% [= 1 − 55.48/1958.34] of the chi-square. Hence both models, especially Model 3, provide a substantial improvement over Model 1. Below, I describe an interpretation of parameters estimated from Model 2 and Model 3.

Interpretation of Parameters Estimated from Model 2

The Effect of Unemployment on Personal Efficacy

In identifying Model 2, the interaction term UEMP*DEP1 was considered but not included in the model because of its insignificance. Hence we can conclude that the effects of unemployment on the transition from low to high personal efficacy and on the reverse transition (i.e., from high to low personal efficacy) have the same absolute magnitude, although they are opposite in sign. In terms of odds ratio, male household heads who experience unemployment in the preceding year are about 0.76 [= exp(−.135 × 2)] times as likely as other male household heads to experience an upgrade in personal efficacy over a one-year period, and are about 1.31 [= exp(.135 × 2)] times as likely as others to experience a downgrade in personal efficacy. The results thus support Hypotheses 5 and 6. (The multiplier 2 is needed because the absence of unemployment is coded as −1 instead of 0; see Table 3.4.)

The Effect of Divorce

The results from Model 2 reveal that, like those of unemployment, the effects of divorce on transitions between the two levels of personal efficacy are the same in absolute magnitude and opposite in sign. This occurs because of the insignificance and subsequent exclusion of DIV*DEP1 from the model.

Compared with others, male household heads who had a divorce in the preceding year are 0.53 [= exp(−.320 × 2)] times as likely to experience an upgrade in personal efficacy, and are 1.90 [= exp(.320 × 2)] times as likely to experience a downgrade in personal efficacy. These results support Hypotheses 3 and 4.

The Relative Effects of Divorce and Unemployment

It was also hypothesized that the effect of divorce on personal efficacy will be stronger than the effect of unemployment because the former is more stressful than the latter. This hypothesis leads to a test for the difference between the effects of DIV and those of UEMP.

Generally, the significance test of the difference between the estimates of two parameters, $\hat{b}_1$ and $\hat{b}_2$ (where $\wedge$ indicates an *estimated* parameter), from a single model can be done by obtaining the estimate of the standard error of the difference, $SE(\hat{b}_1 - \hat{b}_2)$. The variance-covariance matrix of parameter estimates is used such that

$$SE(\hat{b}_1 - \hat{b}_2) = \sqrt{V(\hat{b}_1) + V(\hat{b}_2) - 2Cov(\hat{b}_1, \hat{b}_2)} \qquad (3.9)$$

where V and Cov, respectively, stand for the variance and covariance of parameter estimates. Program BMDPLR, however, prints only the correlation of parameter estimates, rather than covariance of parameter estimates. But the following equality holds true:

$$Cov(\hat{b}_1, \hat{b}_2) = Cor(\hat{b}_1, \hat{b}_2) \times (SE \text{ of } \hat{b}_1) \times (SE \text{ of } \hat{b}_2) \qquad (3.10)$$

where Cor stands for the correlation between two parameter estimates. From the results of the standard errors and the correlation matrix (not presented here), the covariance between the coefficients of DIV and UEMP becomes $(-0.012)(0.0609)(0.0194) = -.000014$. Hence the standard error of the difference between the two coefficients becomes

$$\sqrt{(.0609)^2 + (.0194)^2 - 2(-.000014)} = .0641$$

The Z score for the difference between the effect of DIV and the effect of UEMP then becomes

$$Z = [(-.320) - (-.135)]/(.0641) = -2.89 < -1.96$$

Hence the difference is significant at the 5% level. It implies that the effect of divorce is stronger than the effect of unemployment on the two tendencies, that is, decreased odds of transition from low to high personal efficacy and increased odds of transition from high to low personal efficacy. This supports Hypothesis 7.

The Effects of Time

The presence of DEP1*TIME was tested and found to be insignificant in Model 2, indicating that the effects of time are "symmetric."

The coefficients for the second and third categories of time (years 1971 and 1972) are given in Table 3.5 as −.077 and −.010, respectively. The coefficient for the first category, 1970, becomes −[(−(.077) + (−.010)] = .087. Thus the odds of transition from low to high levels of efficacy decreased from 1970 to 1971 (with odds ratio of 0.85 = exp[−.077 − .087]), and increased somewhat from 1971 to 1972 (with odds ratio of 1.07 = exp[−.010 − (−.077)]). Similarly, the odds of transition from high to low levels increased (with odds ratio of 1.18 = 1.0/0.85) from 1970 to 1971, and somewhat decreased from 1971 to 1972 (with odds ratio of 0.93 = 1/1.07).

The Effects of Duration

The duration effect, DEP2, reveals an interaction with DEP1. Therefore, duration effects need to be described separately for low and high levels of personal efficacy. From Formula 3.8a, the duration effect for the low level of personal efficacy is given by $2[−(.546) + (−.037)] = −1.166$. Hence, compared with subjects who were at the high level of personal efficacy at time $t − 2$ and at the low level of personal efficacy at time $t − 1$, those who were at the low level of personal efficacy at time $t − 2$ as well as time $t − 1$ are 0.31 [= exp(−1.166)] times as likely to upgrade their level of personal efficacy at time t. From Formula 3.8b, the duration effect for the level of high personal efficacy is given by $2[−(.546) − (−.037)] = −1.018$. Hence, compared with subjects who were at the low level of personal efficacy at time $t − 2$ and at the high level of personal efficacy at time $t − 1$, those who were at the high level of personal efficacy at time $t − 2$ as well as time $t − 1$ are 0.36 [= exp(−1.018)] times as likely to downgrade their level of personal efficacy at time t. Thus the interaction effect indicates that the duration effect is slightly stronger for persons at the low level rather than the high level of personal efficacy. The presence of the duration effect itself supports Hypothesis 2.

An Additional Remark on Covariate Effects

Divorce, unemployment, and time all reveal "symmetric" effects on personal efficacy. For any of these covariates, the effect on the transition from the low to high personal efficacy is minus the effect on the reverse transition. This example therefore presents a case where the simultaneous modeling of two-way transitions provides a more parsimonious characterization of covariate effects compared with a separate analysis of the two transitions.

Interpretation of Parameters Estimated from Model 3

Although a parallel analysis can be done for the results of Model 3 regarding the aspects considered for Model 2, the focus below is only on the effects of unemployment and divorce.

The Effect of Unemployment

The main effect for UEMP is the only parameter we need to consider in assessing the effects of unemployment on personal efficacy. Because no interaction effects that include UEMP are significant in Model 3, a consideration of all other possible higher-order interactions does not change the nature of the effect of unemployment on personal efficacy. The parameter estimate for UEMP, -0.133, is similar to that from Model 2 (-0.135). Hence, except for a very minor numerical change, nothing differs regarding the effects of unemployment between the results of Models 2 and 3.

The Effect of Divorce

On the other hand, Model 3 reveals that divorce interacts with two time dimensions (TIME and DEP2). These interactions work differently depending on the direction of transition. Related effects are summarized in Table 3.6.

The results presented in Table 3.6 are derived by first calculating two sums, say, B_1 and B_2, from the main effects and interaction effects that involve DIV. B_1 sums up the coefficients that do not involve interactions with DEP1, that is, the sum of DIV, DIV*DEP2, DIV*TIME, and DIV*DEP2*TIME. B_2 sums up the coefficients that include interactions with DEP1, that is, the sum of DIV*DEP1 and DIV*TIME*DEP1. Then we apply the principle of calculating the effects of a covariate on each direction of transition when the interaction effect with DEP1 is present (see Formula 3.2). We can get the effect of DIV on the transition from low to high personal efficacy by $B_1 - B_2$ and the effect of DIV on the reverse transition by $-(B_1 + B_2)$.

Thus the last column in Table 3.6 (labeled "Total") represents the effects of divorce on personal efficacy. The results in Table 3.6 show that the effects of divorce are far from uniform. Although having a divorce reduces, on the average, the odds of upgrading personal efficacy, one out of six combinations of TIME and DEP2 shows the opposite tendency. Similarly, although having a divorce, on the average, increases the odds of downgrading personal efficacy, one out of

Table 3.6

The Effects of Divorce on Personal Efficacy: Results from Model 3

I. On Transition from Low to High Personal Efficacy

	Main Effect	DIV* DEP2	DIV* TIME[a]	DIV* DEP2* TIME[a]	DIV* DEP1	DIV* DEP1* TIME[a]	Total
(1) Time: 1970							
(a) DEP2=L	[(-.358) -	(-.056) +	.086 -	.419] -	(.012) -	(-.295) =	-.352
(b) DEP2=H	[(-.358) +	(-.056) +	.086 +	.419] -	(.012) -	(-.295) =	.374
(2) Time: 1971							
(a) DEP2=L	[(-.358) -	(-.056) +	(-.119) -	(-.163)] -	(.012) -	(-.082) =	-.188
(b) DEP2=H	[(-.358) +	(-.056) +	(-.119) +	(-.163)] -	(.012) -	(-.082) =	-.626
(3) Time: 1972							
(a) DEP2=L	[(-.358) -	(-.056) +	.033 -	(-.256)] -	(.012) -	.377 =	-.402
(b) DEP2=H	[(-.358) +	(-.056) +	.033 +	(-.256)] -	(.012) -	.377 =	-1.026

II. On Transition from High to Low Personal Efficacy

	Main Effect	DIV* DEP2	DIV* TIME[a]	DIV* DEP2* TIME[a]	DIV* DEP1	DIV* DEP1* TIME[a]	Total
(1) Time: 1970							
(a) DEP2=L	-[(-.358) -	(-.056) +	.086 -	.419] -	(.012) -	(-.295) =	.918
(b) DEP2=H	-[(-.358) +	(-.056) +	.086 +	.419] -	(.012) -	(-.295) =	.192
(2) Time: 1971							
(a) DEP2=L	-[(-.358) -	(-.056) +	(-.119) -	(-.163)] -	(.012) -	(-.082) =	.328
(b) DEP2=H	-[(-.358) +	(-.056) +	(-.119) +	(-.163)] -	(.012) -	(-.082) =	.766
(3) Time: 1972							
(a) DEP2=L	-[(-.358) -	(-.056) +	.033 -	(-.256)] -	(.012) -	.377 =	-.376
(b) DEP2=H	-[(-.358) +	(-.056) +	.033 +	(-.256)] -	(.012) -	.377 =	.248

a. The coefficient for year 1970 is obtained as the negative sum of the coefficients for years 1971 and 1972 because the baseline year 1970 is coded -1 (see Table 3.4).

six combinations of TIME and DEP2 shows the opposite tendency. Even among the effects with the same signs, amounts vary considerably. Hence the results strongly suggest that the effects of having a divorce on personal efficacy vary considerably with individuals and are much less uniform than are the effects of unemployment.

The two combinations where the opposite tendencies were found (TIME = 1970 and DEP2 = H in I; TIME = 1972 and DEP2 = L in II) involve relatively small numbers of divorced subjects (28 and 18, respectively). The opposite effects might have occurred because, for certain cases, the preceding marital discord can be more stressful than divorce, so having a divorce might have a positive effect on mental health. In conclusion, although the effect of divorce on personal efficacy is, on the average, stronger than the effect of unemployment, its effect is much less uniform.

CONCLUDING REMARKS

Although the analysis presented in this chapter is intended to illustrate the flexibility of discrete-time logit models, I admit that the method and models applied in this chapter for the particular dependent variable, personal efficacy, may not be the best ones available. Three major alternatives exist: (a) the use of linear models for panel data analysis, (b) the use of Rasch models, and (c) the use of the Liang-Zeger method for panel data with the logit model (Bye & Riley, 1989; Liang & Zeger, 1986). The first alternative permits the use of the interval-scale version of personal efficacy and allows the introduction of a random error term that is autocorrelated across waves. The second alternative, the use of Rasch models, is effective only if the time-lagged effect of personal efficacy is due solely to unobserved population heterogeneity.[5] Under this assumption, the method can assess the effects of covariates, controlling for unobserved population heterogeneity. (For examples in the use of Rasch models, see Duncan, 1984a, 1984b, 1985a.) These two alternatives are better than the present method with regard to the modeling of uncontrolled heterogeneity. The third alternative, the use of the Liang-Zeger method, can handle nonindependence of observations across waves. But since the method treats correlated errors across waves as a nuisance, it is not suitable in modeling time dependence and its interactions with covariates. Consequently, all three alternatives lose the benefits of simultaneously modeling the determinants of upward and downward transitions in personal efficacy.

A further elaboration of the present method is possible. The technique that improves upon the present method, while retaining the discrete-time event history approach to the analysis of personal efficacy, is a model that introduces into the logit model a set of time-specific random error terms that are autocorrelated across discrete time points for each subject. Although the technique for including the random error term into the logit model has been introduced in the literature (Allison, 1987; Amemiya & Nold, 1975; Chamberlain, 1980), it has not yet been incorporated into any computer program for the analysis of event history data.

Readers who need to know more about the method described in this chapter may refer to Heckman (1981) and Yamaguchi (1990b). For an alternative approach to the panel-data analysis of two-way transitions, see Coleman (1981, chap. 3). A longitudinal analysis of personal efficacy using the PSID data is reported by Lachman (1985).

PROBLEMS

(1) Using the data in Table 3.2, reproduce the results of Table 3.5.

(2) Redo the analysis using only the data for time 2 and time 3 in Table 3.1. Obtain the best-fitting proportional odds model and the best-fitting model among those that do not impose zero marginal frequencies. Use the stepwise regression and the 1% criterion for omission and removal of factors. Interpret the parameter estimated from the first and the second models with respect to the effects of DIV, UEMP, DEP2, and TIME.

NOTES

1. Models introduced by Heckman and Borjas (1980) go beyond this characterization of interdependence among spells. These authors introduce a set of spell-specific random error terms that are autocorrelated across spells (see also Flinn & Heckman, 1982).

2. The methodology proposed by Liang and Zeger (1986) handles observations that are not independent, and the application of the method to logit models (Bye & Riley, 1989) overcomes this limitation. See this chapter's concluding remarks for a further discussion of the Liang-Zeger method.

3. However, it is also true that time-lagged effects are not likely to disappear completely as time goes back. I believe that this occurs as the time-lagged effects capture the effects of uncontrolled population heterogeneity. It follows that the model will be improved greatly by including a random error term to reflect population heterogeneity. The present application relies on the standard logistic regression program, which cannot take this into account. See the chapter's concluding remarks for a related discussion.

4. See note 3.

5. For the analysis of panel data, Duncan (1985b) has proposed a model that introduces a Markovianlike effect into the Rasch model at the level of aggregate data. Although the idea has merit, it does not exactly correspond to an individual-level response model that reflects both latent individual traits and the Markovian dependence on the previous response.

4

Log-Rate Models for Piecewise Constant Rates

M E T H O D S   A N D   M O D E L S

This chapter discusses log-rate models for piecewise constant rates. It is assumed that hazard rates are *piecewise constant*, that is, constant *within* each interval of a set of time intervals. Hazard rates are not necessarily constant across time intervals. Since the piecewise constant rate implies that the probability density function of duration is piecewise exponential, the models described here are referred to as *piecewise exponential models* as well as *piecewise constant rate models*. Although hazard rates are free to vary only across time intervals, the models assume that hazards exist continuously over time. The application of log-linear analysis for piecewise exponential models described in this chapter follows from the work of Holford (1980) and Laird and Olivier (1981).

In log-rate models, a set of time categories defines the duration of the risk period. The time categories form the major time dimension for modeling the event of interest. For example, in the case of marriage, age is the major time dimension under the assumption that subjects enter the risk period at a certain same age. In the case of divorce and job separation, duration of marriage and duration of job are, respectively, the major time dimensions. However, we may also combine the major time dimension with another time dimension to define a two-dimensional set of cross-classified time categories. For example, if we have longitudinal data of multiple cohorts, age and period may both be used to define the time intervals in the analysis of marriage.

We assume that hazard rates vary among heterogeneous groups, and that group differences can be characterized by a set of time-independent categorical explanatory variables. We also assume that the logarithm of hazard rates is a linear function of parameters for time and other explanatory variables. It follows that the parameters represent the effects of the explanatory variables on log-rates.

By analyzing piecewise constant rates with log-rate models, we can apply a standard program for log-linear analysis. Specifically, we can obtain the chi-square statistic G^2 to test the fit of each model with the data and compare nested models. In particular, the group of log-rate models thus formulated includes both proportional hazards models (defined later) and nonproportional hazards models as its special cases. A comparison between nested proportional and nonproportional hazards models leads to a test of nonproportionality.

In the following, I assume that there are no left-censored observations.

Log-Rate Models for Piecewise Constant Rates

Saturated Log-Rate Model

Let me describe log-rate models by using a model with three variables. One variable is the time variable and the other two are time-independent categorical variables. Then, the *saturated* model can be expressed as follows:

$$\ln (F_{tij}^{TAB}/W_{tij}^{TAB}) = \lambda + \lambda_t^T + \lambda_i^A + \lambda_j^B + \lambda_{ti}^{TA} + \lambda_{tj}^{TB} + \lambda_{ij}^{AB} + \lambda_{tij}^{TAB} \quad (4.1)$$

where T is the time variable, and A and B are time-independent categorical variables. F_{tij}^{TAB} is the expected frequency of events for cell (t, i, j) in the cross-classification table, and W_{tij}^{TAB} is the total amount of exposure to the risk of having the event during the time interval t for group (i, j). Thus the ratio of the two factors, $F_{tij}^{TAB} / W_{tij}^{TAB}$, becomes the *rate* of the occurrence of the event during time interval t for group (i, j). It follows that Formula 4.1 specifies *log-rates* as a linear function of parameters.

Each set of lambda parameters satisfies a standard set of linear constraints, such that the sum of parameters across categories of a variable is zero for each possible combination of categories for other variables. The constraints are thus given as follows:

$$\sum_t \lambda_t^T = \sum_i \lambda_i^A = \sum_j \lambda_j^B = 0; \qquad \sum_t \lambda_{ti}^{TA} = \sum_i \lambda_{ti}^{TA} = 0;$$

$$\sum_t \lambda_{tj}^{TB} = \sum_j \lambda_{tj}^{TB} = 0; \qquad \sum_i \lambda_{ij}^{AB} = \sum_j \lambda_{ij}^{AB} = 0; \qquad (4.2)$$

$$\sum_t \lambda_{tij}^{TAB} = \sum_i \lambda_{tij}^{TAB} = \sum_j \lambda_{tij}^{TAB} = 0$$

It follows from these constraints that the estimate of lambda for the last category of each variable (such as A) for each set of lambda parameters that includes this variable (such as λ_i^A, λ_{ti}^{TA}, λ_{ij}^{AB}, and λ_{tij}^{TAB}) is calculated as minus the sum of other estimated lambda parameters within each set. Examples of this calculation are given later.

In Formula 4.1, the constant lambda, λ, represents the average level of log-rate. Parameters λ_t^T, λ_i^A and λ_j^B respectively represent the main effects of variable T, A, and B on log-rates. Parameters λ_{ti}^{TA}, λ_{tj}^{TB} and λ_{ij}^{AB} respectively represent the interaction effects of T by A, T by B, and A by B on log-rates. Finally, parameter λ_{tij}^{TAB} represents the three-factor interaction effects of T by A by B on log-rates.

The model given in Formula 4.1 is *saturated* because it includes all possible higher-order interactions among categorical explanatory variables. It uses as many parameters as the number of cells in the table of cross-classified frequency of events. Hence it always fits the data perfectly. On the other hand, we can construct *unsaturated hierarchical log-rate models* by omitting some sets of lambda parameters systematically, as described below.

Hierarchical Log-Rate Models, Proportional Hazards Models, and Nonproportional Hazards Models

Hierarchical log-rate models take into account the order among interaction effects in hypothesizing the absence or presence of the sets of lambda parameters. For instance, if a model hypothesizes the interaction effect between two variables, the model also includes the main effects for each of the two component variables involved in the interaction effect. If a model hypothesizes a three-factor interaction effect, all combinations of lower-order effects—that is, two-factor interaction effects and main effects—among component variables must be present. Suppose that we always retain in the model the main effect of time T. Then, 14 hierarchical log-rate models, including the saturated model, can be identified as models with three variables T, A, and B. They are depicted in Figure 4.1.

In Figure 4.1, (TAB) represents the saturated model; $(TA)(TB)(AB)$ represents the model in which the three-factor interaction effect is hypothesized to be absent, and all effects of lower order (i.e., interaction effects and main effects) are hypothesized to be present; each of the next three models—that is, models $(TA)(AB)$, $(TA)(TB)$, and $(TB)(AB)$—includes two out of three interaction effects between two variables as well as the main effects of all three variables; each of the

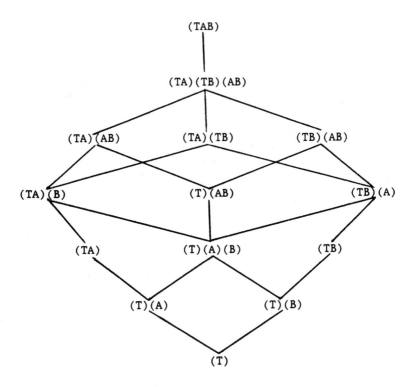

Figure 4.1. Hierarchical Log-Rate Models with Three Variables (Time, A, and B), Assuming the Presence of Time Effects

next three models—models $(TA)(B)$, $(T)(AB)$, and $(TB)(A)$—includes only one out of the three interaction effects between two variables as well as the main effects of all three variables; model $(T)(A)(B)$ includes only the main effects of three variables; models (TA) and (TB) include the interaction effect of time and one explanatory variable in addition to their main effects, and hypothesize the absence of the effect of the other explanatory variable; models $(T)(A)$ and $(T)(B)$ hypothesize the main effects of only two variables, one of which is time; and, finally, model (T) hypothesizes only the main effect of time and the absence of the effects of explanatory variables A and B.

Figure 4.1 also depicts the hierarchy among models. Recall that the likelihood-ratio test for the relative goodness of fit between models requires that (a) the models to be compared are nested and (b) the model with more parameters than the other fits the data adequately. For example, model *(TA)(AB)* cannot be compared with models *(TA)(TB)*, *(TB)(AB)*, *(TB)(A)*, or *(TB)*, but may be compared with other models if either model *(TA)(AB)* or the other model fits the data.

If the model does not include any interaction effects of time and other variables on log-rates—that is, if $\lambda_{ti}^{TA} = \lambda_{tj}^{TB} = \lambda_{tij}^{TAB} = 0$ is hypothesized in Formula 4.1—we have a *proportional hazards model*. The proportional hazards model hypothesizes that ratios of hazard rates among different groups are constant over time. On the other hand, if an interaction effect of time and another variable is included in the model, such as λ_{ti}^{TA} or λ_{tj}^{TB} in Formula 4.1, we have a *nonproportional hazards model*. Among the 14 models given in Figure 4.1, models *(T)(AB)*, *(T)(A)(B)*, *(T)(A)*, *(T)(B)*, and *(T)* are proportional hazards models and the other 9 models are nonproportional hazards models.

Thus the first step in model selection involves a search for a hierarchical log-rate model that fits the data most parsimoniously. A second step for attaining a parsimoniously fitting model is usually important, however. This step is concerned with the modeling of time dependence and of the interaction effect of time and other variables, which is discussed next.

Modeling Time Dependence

Generally, there are three distinct approaches to modeling time dependence. Here the term *approach* implies combining a method with a group of models. One approach is parametric. We assume that the form of time dependence is characterized by a specific function of time. The simplest models of this kind introduce only one parameter to characterize time dependence. The Gompertz and Weibull models are one-parameter models that can be defined, respectively, as follows:

$$\text{Gompertz:} \quad \ln[\text{h}(t)] = a + \sum_i b_i X_i + ct \tag{4.2a}$$

$$\text{Weibull:} \quad \ln[\text{h}(t)] = a + \sum_i b_i X_i + c[\ln(t)] \tag{4.2b}$$

where $\text{h}(t)$ is the hazard rate, a is the constant parameter, b_i are parameters for explanatory variables X_i (where $i = 1, \ldots, I$), and c is the parameter for time dependence. We can generalize the Gompertz and Weibull models by hypothesizing the effects of higher powers of t or $\ln(t)$. For example, ct can be replaced by $c_1 t + c_2 t^2$, and $c[\ln(t)]$ can be replaced by $c_1[\ln(t)] + c_2[\ln(t)]^2$.

Although the Gompertz and Weibull models and their extensions assume that hazard rates change continuously with time, these models can be approximated with log-rate models by applying a step-functional characterization for t or $\ln(t)$. The procedure is described in the application presented later.

The second approach was introduced by Cox (1972, 1975) for proportional hazards models and uses the partial likelihood method for parameter estimation. This approach to modeling time dependence is nonparametric because it does not require any specific parametric characterization of the baseline hazard function (which will be defined in the next chapter). This approach is especially popular in demographic research. The partial likelihood method and related models will be discussed in Chapters 6 and 7.

The third approach to modeling time dependence is also nonparametric. It can be effectively employed for log-rate models discussed in this chapter and discrete-time models that were discussed in the preceding two chapters. In this approach, which is based on the maximum likelihood method, dummy variables are used to distinguish a discrete set of time points or time intervals. Parameters for the dummy variables are estimated, thereby characterizing time dependence without specifying its functional form. For example, the lambda parameters, λ_t^T, in Formula 4.1 make a nonparametric characterization of time dependence.

As we will discover throughout the applications presented in this book, the pattern of time dependence in empirical data does not conform to a specific functional form in many cases. Hence, unless researchers test the goodness of fit of the model that has a parametric characterization for time dependence and confirm that the model has a good fit with the data, a parametric characterization of time dependence is not recommended. However, the interaction effects of time and other explanatory variables may more often be characterized adequately by using a specific time function.

Generally, when researchers test nonproportional hazards models by hypothesizing interaction effects of time and explanatory variables on log-rates, they again have a choice between a nonparametric and a parametric characterization of the interaction effects. In fact, the choice can be determined by the likelihood-ratio test.

The interaction effects between time and a categorical explanatory variable A in Formula 4.1, λ_{ti}^{TA}, employ a nonparametric characterization for the effects. The effects may be replaced by one of the following parametric characterizations to test whether the interaction effects can be modeled more parsimoniously.

$$\alpha_i^A t \tag{4.3a}$$

$$\alpha_i^A [\ln(t)] \tag{4.3b}$$

where α_i^A are parameters that satisfy $\Sigma_i \alpha_i^A = 0$, and t and $\ln(t)$ are scores defined for time categories. If it is necessary, we can also include in the model the interaction effects involving higher powers of t or $\ln(t)$, such as $\beta_i^A t^2$ in Formula 4.3a and $\beta_i^A [\ln(t)]^2$ in Formula 4.3b, where $\Sigma_i \beta_i^A = 0$. While the full interactions λ_{ti}^{TA} employ $(N_T - 1)(N_A - 1)$ parameters, where N_T and N_A are the number of categories for time and variable A, respectively, the use of α_i^A in Formula 4.3a or 4.3b employs only $(N_A - 1)$ parameters.[1]

Notes on Input Data

For log-rate models, we need a pair of data sets (i.e., the number of events and the amount of exposure to risk) for each cell of a cross-classification by a categorical time variable and a set of categorical time-independent variables. The calculation of the number of events, such as the number of job separations during each time interval among sample subjects having a set of time-independent characteristics, can be done in a straightforward manner. On the other hand, the calculation of the amount of exposure to risk involves the calculation of two quantities:

(1) the number of persons at risk for having the event at the beginning of each time period
(2) an estimate for the average amount of exposure to risk during each time period

The expected average amount of exposure normally depends on whether (a) the event occurred during the time period, (b) the observation was censored during the time period, or (c) the subject survived to the end of the time period. For each combination of categories for time and other explanatory variables, the total amount of exposure to risk becomes the sum of the products of quantities 1 and 2, summed across cases a-c. This procedure is described in detail later with an example.

Specification of Rate Data in Log-Linear Analysis

In this chapter, the SPSS-LOGLINEAR program is used for the illustrative analysis. We can employ several programs for log-linear analysis, such as SAS-CATMOD, FREQ, and GLIM, for the same purpose. In the SPSS-LOGLINEAR program, we can specify *cell weights* by a statement CWEIGHT=W, where W is the variable that represents cell weight. Let F_i be the frequency of events expected from a given model for cell i, and let W_i be the cell weight that is assigned for cell i. When cell weights are specified, $\ln(F_i/W_i)$ rather than $\ln(F_i)$ is modeled. It follows that we can obtain log-rate models when the cell weights represent the amount of exposure to risk for each cell.

The log-rate models treat the estimated amounts of exposure to risk—that is, W_i—as *fixed* weights. Thus we are conditioning the equation on the values of the exposure estimates.

APPLICATION:
AN ANALYSIS OF INTERFIRM JOB MOBILITY

Data and Hypotheses

In this section, I present the analysis of interfirm job mobility in Japan using the 1975 Social Stratification and Mobility Survey (Grusky, 1983; Tominaga, 1979; Yamaguchi, 1987b). The subjects used here are a sample of male employees aged 20-64 in 1975. For each sample subject, the survey collected the age of first entry into employment, the age of leaving the employer, and age at the survey date. Hence for subjects who left their first employers we have information on the age at which the event occurred, that is, an interfirm job separation. For subjects who did not leave their first employers, we have information about the age at which censoring by the survey occurred.

In the analysis presented below, we will be concerned with the duration of employment up to 30 years to avoid confounding interfirm job separations due to retirement or the anticipation of retirement with other interfirm job separations.[2] It follows that subjects who worked more than 30 years for their first employers are treated as having their duration of employment censored at the end of their thirtieth year of employment.

In the illustrative analysis presented in this chapter, I include firm size at the time the subject entered the firm as the only time-independent explanatory variable. Hence the present analysis is limited regarding the control for heterogeneity by explanatory variables. A more elaborate multivariate analysis for the same dependent event will be presented in the next chapter using the Cox method. The analysis described in this chapter, however, accomplishes two things that cannot be done in the analysis described in Chapter 5: (a) the goodness-of-fit chi-square tests for models and (b) the modeling of time dependence and a comparison among alternative models of time dependence.

There is a substantive reason for the choice of firm size as the explanatory variable. The literature on Japanese labor markets indicates that firm size is a major indicator of labor market segmentation in Japan. Three specific hypotheses can be advanced.

First, it is known that large private firms and government agencies have a so-called lifetime employment system in which their regular employees are neither fired nor laid off. This system does not apply to small firms (Cole, 1979). Hence we expect the following:

- *Hypothesis 1*: The rate of job separations will be significantly larger for small private firms than for large private firms and government agencies.

Other theories consider the lifetime employment system and the seniority-based wage system of Japan to be a type of internal labor market (Cole, 1973; Koike, 1983; Sumiya, 1974a, 1974b). In order to avoid the costs of retraining, firms attempt to retain workers who have acquired firm-specific skills through on-the-job training. On the average, employees of large private firms are more likely than employees of small private firms to have on-the-job training and to acquire firm-specific skills. If these theories hold true, then we expect the following:

- *Hypothesis 2:* There will be a sharper decline in the rate of interfirm job separations as a function of duration of employment among employees of large private firms than among those of small private firms.

This hypothesis leads to a test of a specific interaction effect of firm size and duration on the rates of job separations.

Finally, it is also known that, compared to large private firms, government agencies in Japan have a more rigid salary scale based on tenure. Consequently, compared with employees of large private firms, government workers have lower initial salaries, but the income return for tenure is larger. This fact leads us to expect the following:

- *Hypothesis 3:* Government employees will have a higher rate of job separation at early duration periods, but the decline of the rate with duration of employment will be sharper compared with employees of large private firms.

This again leads to a test of a specific interaction effect of firm type/size and duration on the rates of interfirm job separations.

A test of these three hypotheses is presented below. The analysis presented below also addresses methodological concerns by providing detailed descriptions of (a) the calculation of the amount of exposure to risk, (b) the construction and testing of models, (c) a comparison of nested models, and (d) the interpretation of parameters estimated from models.

Calculation of Input Data, I:
The Numbers of Events, Censored Observations,
and Sample Survivors

Table 4.1 presents frequency data for both the occurrences of the event and censored observations, as a function of (a) the age difference between the event's occurrence or censoring versus entry into employment and (b) firm size. The third panel of Table 4.1 presents the number of sample survivors (which is derived from the first and second data sets, as described below). The first and second data sets of Table 4.1 show, for example, that one person left a government job during the same age as that of employment (row 0 and column 6 for the number of events), and five persons whose ages are two years older than their age of employment were holding their first jobs with the government at the survey date (row 2 and column 6 of the number of censored observations).

For each given category of firm size ($i = 1, \ldots, 6$) and duration ($t = 0, \ldots, 30$), we define the following terms:

N_t : the number of subjects who had the event during the tth time period

C_t : the number of subjects whose observation was censored during the tth time period

S_t : the number of subjects who were at risk of having the event at the beginning of the tth time period (This number is referred to as the number of *sample survivors.*)

It follows that

$$S_{t+1} = S_t - (N_t + C_t) \qquad (4.4)$$

holds true. Note that Formula 4.4 indicates that, given the number of sample survivors at the beginning of the risk period $t = 0$, sample survivors at each time period $t \geq 1$ can be calculated from knowledge of N_t and C_t. Similarly, if we know the number of sample survivors at the end of the last risk period (e.g., $t = 30$), S_t can be sequentially calculated in reverse order as $S_{t+1} + (N_t + C_t)$.

Calculation of Input Data, II:
The Amount of Exposure to Risk

Given the three data sets, denoted by N_t, C_t, and S_t, we can calculate the amount of exposure to risk for each cell in the cross-classification of duration by firm size. For this calculation, we assume that events and censored observations are uniformly distributed within each time period. It follows that subjects who had either the event or censoring during a time interval are at risk for having the event for one half the length of the interval, on the average. In the current analysis, then, each of $(N_t + C_t)$ subjects has an average risk period of 6 months and each of S_{t+1} subjects has a risk period of 12 months during each time period $t = 1, \ldots, 30$. It follows that for the tth time period, the total amount of exposure to risk W_t, as expressed in months, is

$$W_t = 6(N_t + C_t) + 12\,S_{t+1} \qquad t = 1, \ldots, 30 \qquad (4.5)$$

During the time period $t = 0$ the age of the event/censoring is the same as the age of employment. However, since subjects do not enter the risk period (i.e., employment) on their birth dates (i.e., the beginning of the age of employment), we need to make an additional assumption regarding the distribution of times of entry into the risk period during the age of employment. If we assume that entries into the risk period are uniformly distributed during the age, and that the risk of having an event is constant during one year after entry, then

Table 4.1

Number of Events, Censored Observations, Survivors in the Sample as a Function of Firm Size and the Difference Between the Age at Entry into the First Job and Age at the Occurrence of First Interfirm Job Separation/Censoring (male employees aged 20-64 in 1975 in Japan)

Age Difference	Number of Events Firm Size[a]						Number of Censored Observations Firm Size[a]						Number of Survivors in the Sample Firm Size[a]					
	1	2	3	4	5	6	1	2	3	4	5	6	1	2	3	4	5	6
0	7	7	9	6	4	1	0	1	1	1	2	6	154	408	390	186	406	237
1	15	45	30	17	22	20	0	0	2	2	4	3	147	400	380	179	400	230
2	11	51	47	19	27	16	0	3	3	3	6	5	132	355	348	160	374	207
3	18	46	34	22	28	20	2	3	8	2	13	2	121	301	298	138	341	186
4	21	36	28	7	20	15	0	5	6	4	8	5	101	252	256	114	300	164
5	21	31	22	10	24	12	3	2	5	3	10	1	80	211	222	103	272	144
6	13	18	16	7	11	4	0	3	7	2	5	1	56	178	195	90	238	131
7	5	17	17	8	4	7	1	6	13	8	7	3	43	157	172	81	222	126
8	8	11	7	4	3	9	0	11	8	6	9	4	37	134	142	65	211	116
9	6	10	6	2	3	4	1	5	7	3	9	3	29	112	127	55	199	103
10	3	11	12	2	13	4	0	6	5	2	11	8	22	97	114	50	187	96
11	0	4	2	2	6	1	1	0	4	1	10	5	19	80	97	46	163	84
12	2	5	5	3	9	1	1	2	5	4	5	1	18	76	91	43	147	78
13	1	2	3	0	3	0	0	3	5	3	7	3	15	69	81	36	133	76
14	0	1	3	1	2	2	2	3	4	0	8	5	14	64	73	33	123	73
15	1	5	3	0	2	0	1	4	4	2	6	6	12	60	66	32	113	66
16	0	3	2	0	2	1	0	0	6	2	7	2	10	51	59	30	105	60
17	0	5	1	0	2	2	0	3	4	4	4	3	10	48	51	28	96	57
18	0	2	1	1	2	4	0	1	6	1	6	3	10	40	46	24	90	52
19	1	3	3	3	2	0	1	3	7	3	6	2	10	37	39	22	82	45

Duration																		
20	43	74	16	29	31	8	0	5	0	4	3	0	0	1	0	2	1	2
21	43	68	15	23	27	6	0	4	0	1	5	0	1	3	1	1	0	0
22	42	61	15	21	22	6	4	5	1	2	2	2	1	1	0	0	3	0
23	37	55	14	19	17	4	1	4	1	0	4	1	0	0	0	0	0	0
24	36	51	13	19	13	3	6	3	2	3	1	0	1	3	0	0	0	0
25	29	45	11	16	12	3	3	5	1	1	1	0	0	0	1	1	1	1
26	26	40	9	15	10	2	6	4	1	2	0	1	0	0	0	0	0	0
27	20	36	8	12	10	2	5	3	0	1	0	0	1	0	0	0	0	0
28	14	33	8	11	10	1	2	3	1	1	0	0	0	1	1	0	0	0
29	12	29	6	10	10	1	1	2	0	0	0	0	0	0	0	1	0	0
30	11	27	6	9	10	1	0	4	0	1	0	0	0	1	1	1	0	0
	11	22	5	7	10	1	11]^b	22	5	7	10	[1						

SOURCE: 1975 Social Stratification and Mobility Survey in Japan.
a. Number of employees: 1 = 0-4; 2 = 5-29; 3 = 30-299; 4 = 300-999; 5 = 1,000 and more; 6 = government.
b. The number of cases censored because they have reached the upper limit of the 30-year duration period.

we obtain the expected duration of the risk period for the age of employment as four months for cases in which employment was terminated either by a job separation or by censoring before the end of this age. (See the appendix to this chapter for a proof.) For cases where subjects survived until the end of the age of employment, the expected duration of the risk period for the age of employment becomes approximately six months, given an additional condition that the probability of having the event during this period is much smaller than one. (See the appendix for this proof as well.) It follows that the amount of exposure to risk, in months, for the period zero can be estimated as

$$W_0 = 4(N_0 + C_0) + 6S_1 \qquad (4.6)$$

Note that although Formulas 4.5 and 4.6 are adequate for the present application and many other similar cases, they are not applicable to all situations. The calculation of W_i depends on the assumptions regarding the distributions of times for entries into the risk set, occurrences of events, and censoring during time intervals. In some cases, the assumption of uniform distributions employed here may not be adequate. For example, if entry into employment were expressed by year of employment instead of age of employment, the assumption would be inadequate for the distribution of entries into employment among Japanese new employees because the majority of them are known to start working in a particular month, namely, April.

See Namboodiri and Suchindran (1987) for further discussion of the calculation of exposure to risk.

Notes on Combining Categories

If the distribution of events is sparse, the chi-square statistics will be less accurate[3] and/or zero marginal frequencies, which we may wish to avoid, may exist. Therefore, we may consider collapsing some adjacent time periods. When time categories are collapsed, both the number of events N_t and the amount of exposure to risk W_t simply need to be summed across categories. If time periods need to be collapsed, this should be done after the calculation of the amount of exposure to risk for each time period in which the data of N_t and C_t are available. If time categories are collapsed first, the estimates for the amount of exposure to risk become less accurate.[4]

Table 4.2

Number of Events and the Amount of Exposure to Risk by Firm Size
and Period of Risk (male employees aged 20-64 in 1975 in Japan)

Risk period			Number of Events Firm Size Category						The Amount of Exposure to the Risk in Person-Months Firm Size Category				
	1	2	3	4	5	6	1	2	3	4	5	6
0	7	7	9	6	4	1	910	2432	2320	1102	2424	1408
1	15	45	30	17	22	20	1674	4530	4368	2034	4644	2622
2	11	51	47	19	27	16	1518	3936	3876	1788	4290	2358
3	18	46	34	22	28	20	1332	3318	3324	1512	3846	2100
4	21	36	28	7	20	15	1086	2778	2868	1302	3432	1848
5	21	31	22	10	24	12	816	2334	2502	1158	3060	1650
6	13	18	16	7	11	4	594	2010	2202	1026	2760	1542
7	5	17	17	8	4	7	480	1746	1884	876	2598	1452
8	8	11	7	4	3	9	396	1476	1614	720	2460	1314
9	6	10	6	2	3	4	306	1254	1446	630	2316	1194
10	3	11	12	2	13	4	246	1062	1266	576	2100	1080
11	0	4	2	2	6	1	222	936	1128	534	1860	972
12	2	5	5	3	9	1	198	870	1032	474	1680	924
13-14	1	3	6	1	5	2	330	1542	1758	804	2952	1728
15-16	1	8	5	0	4	1	252	1260	1410	720	2514	1458
17-18	0	7	2	1	4	6	242	990	1092	588	2148	1236
19-22	3	7	7	4	7	2	324	1284	1494	768	3258	2028
23-26	1	1	1	1	3	1	132	582	786	528	2178	1434
27-30	0	0	2	2	2	1	54	480	474	318	1416	630

NOTE: See Table 4.1 for firm size categories. Data in this table are derived from data in Table 4.1.

For the data in Table 4.1, time periods 13 and 14, 15 and 16, 17 and 18, periods from 19 to 22, those from 23 to 26, and those from 27 to 30 are combined. For each new time category, the results for N_t and W_t by firm size are given in Table 4.2.

The pair of data sets of N_{ti} and W_{ti}, where i denotes firm size, are used as the input data for the analysis of log-rates presented below.

Programming of Models

For log-rate models, we cannot test Gompertz or Weibull models exactly. While the log-rate models assume piecewise constancy of hazard rates, the Gompertz and Weibull models assume a continuous change in hazard rates as a function of time. Hence we employ a step-functional approximation for the Gompertz-type or Weibull-type duration dependence. The approximation is straightforward for the Gompertz-type duration dependence. For each discrete time interval, we can assign a midpoint score of duration for the interval and assume that log-rates depend linearly on scores. We can generalize this model by introducing the dependence of rates on the quadratic term or higher-order powers of the scores.

Such an approximation may not be as good for the Weibull-type duration dependence. Since the log-rates become a function of $\ln(t)$, the increment in log-rates for a one-unit increase in t is not constant. Furthermore, the variability in the values of $\ln(t)$ is great in the time interval $(0, 1)$. Hence we have no appropriate score to assign for this particular time interval. In this chapter, the Weibull-type duration dependence is approximated with a pair of variables. One variable assigns a score of $\ln(t)$ to the time interval that has a midpoint duration of t. The second variable is a dummy variable for the period "zero." This variable adjusts the level of baseline hazard when the age of employment equals the age of separation from the employer.

Table 4.3 presents the SPSS-LOGLINEAR program used for the analysis. The statements in the program are described step by step below.

The first line in Table 4.3, the DATA LIST statement, indicates that the input data fall between the BEGIN DATA and END DATA statements; the data follow a free (LIST) format with one case per record. Four variables—F, D, JBSP, and RISK—are read. Variables F and D indicate the category of firm size and employment duration, respectively; variable JBSP represents the number of job separations for each combined state of F and D variables; and variable RISK represents the amount of exposure to risk for the corresponding state.

The second line, WEIGHT BY JBSP, indicates that each record is to be weighted by the value given by variable JBSP. Since the data are aggregated, each record does not represent one observation. The number of occurrences of the event that each record represents is given by the variable JBSP.

Variable DR, as defined in lines 3 and 4, represents the linear effect of duration on log hazard rates. The variable DR is assigned the value of the midpoint for each time interval of duration. Note that the thirteenth period gets a score of 13.5, because this time period represents the combined duration of 13 and 14 years. Similarly, the seventeenth period gets a score of 24.5 because it represents durations of 23 to 26 years. The period zero gets a score of 0.25 because the

Table 4.3

SPSS Program for the Analysis of Data in Table 4.2

	line[a]
DATA LIST LIST / F D JBSP RISK	1
WEIGHT BY JBSP	2
COMPUTE DR=D	3
RECODE DR (0=0.25)(13=13.5)(14=15.5)(15=17.5)(16=20.5)(17=24.5)(18=28.5)	4
COMPUTE DR2=DR**2	5
COMPUTE LDR=D	6
RECODE LDR (0=1)(13=13.5)(14=15.5)(15=17.5)(16=20.5)(17=24.5)(18=28.5)	7
COMPUTE LDR=LN(LDR)	8
COMPUTE LDR2=LDR**2	9
COMPUTE D0=D	10
RECODE D0 (0=1)(1 THRU 18=0)	11
COMPUTE X=1	12
LOGLINEAR F(1,6) D(0,18) WITH DR DR2 LDR LDR2 D0 X/	13
CWEIGHT=RISK/	14
PRINT=ESTIM/	15
/* CONSTANT RATE MODELS	16
DESIGN=X/	17
DESIGN=F/	18
/* PARAMETRIC DURATION MODELS	19
/* PROPORTIONAL HAZARDS MODELS	20
DESIGN=DR/	21
DESIGN=DR, DR2/	22
DESIGN=D0, LDR/	23
DESIGN=D0, LDR, LDR2/	24
DESIGN=F, DR/	25
DESIGN=F, DR, DR2/	26
DESIGN=F, D0, LDR/	27
DESIGN=F, D0, LDR, LDR2/	28
/* NON-PROPORTIONAL HAZARDS MODELS	29
DESIGN=F, DR, F BY DR/	30
DESIGN=F, DR, DR2, F BY DR/	31
DESIGN=F, DR, DR2, F BY DR, F BY DR2/	32
DESIGN=F, D0, LDR, F BY LDR/	33
DESIGN=F, D0, LDR, LDR2, F BY LDR/	34
DESIGN=F, D0, LDR, LDR2, F BY LDR, F BY LDR2/	35
/* NON-PARAMETRIC DURATION MODELS	36
/* PROPORTIONAL HAZARDS MODELS	37
DESIGN=D/	38
DESIGN=F, D/	39
/* NON-PROPORTIONAL HAZARDS MODELS	40
DESIGN=F, D, F BY DR/	41
DESIGN=F, D, F BY DR, F BY DR2/	42

Continued

Table 4.3, Continued

	line[a]
DESIGN=F, D, F by LDR/	43
DESIGN=F, D, F by LDR, F by LDR2/	44
BEGIN DATA	45
(data omitted)	.
END DATA	.

a. Line numbers do not appear in the program.

expected duration for those who survive to the end of the period is approximately half a year (see the appendix to this chapter) and, therefore, the midpoint of duration becomes approximately one fourth of a year.

Another variable, LDR, is defined in lines 7-9. It gets a score equal to the logarithm of the mid-duration score, except in the period zero, for which it gets a score of 0 instead of ln(0.25). The score 0 is arbitrary here because we simultaneously include covariate D0 in the model. Lines 10-11 define a dummy covariate D0 that, when combined with covariate LDR, reflects the deviation of the observed rate from the rate expected from LDR at the period zero. The use of both LDR and D0 means that we hypothesize only a constant time effect for the period zero, without specifying its amount.

The LOGLINEAR statement in line 13 defines the dimension of the cross-classified data to be analyzed. It identifies a two-way cross-classification by variables F and D here. The value range of variables are also specified respectively as (1, 6) and (0, 18). Variables that follow the WITH option in the LOGLINEAR statement are "covariates," in the program's terminology, each of which takes a specified set of values for cells of the table. Here, DR, DR2, D0, LDR, and LDR2 are specified as covariates. They vary only across time categories and are invariant across firm-size categories.

The statement that appears in line 14, CWEIGHT=RISK, distinguishes the log-rate model from the conventional log-linear model. This statement commands the LOGLINEAR procedure to model ln(JBSP/RISK), which is the logarithm of the *rate* of job separation, instead of modeling ln(JBSP), which is the logarithm of *frequency* of job separations.

Each DESIGN statement specifies a distinct model. Lines 17 and 18 specify constant rate models. One model is constant and independent of firm size (line 17), while the other is constant for each firm-size category (line 18).

From lines 21-35, 14 distinct models are defined, each of which hypothesizes a certain parametric characterization for duration dependence. The first 8 models (lines 21-28) are proportional hazards models that include either duration effects only (no effects of firm size) or a combination of duration effects and the main effects of firm size. The next 6 models (lines 30-35) are nonproportional hazards models that include interaction effects of duration and firm size.

Nonparametric duration models are defined in lines 37-44. Recall that nonparametric duration models reflect any shape of duration dependence by a step-function. The models in Table 4.3 characterize the duration dependence with a set of 18 lambda parameters for 19 time periods. The first two models, defined in lines 38-39, are proportional hazards models, and the next four models, defined in lines 41-44, are nonproportional hazards models. Since this is an analysis of a two-way table, a full set of interactions between firm size and duration leads to a saturated model. Hence the interaction effects of firm size and duration are formulated by using parametric characterizations for duration, that is, using DR, DR2, LDR, and LDR2.

In the programming of models based on SPSS-LOGLINEAR, the difference between the nonparametric and parametric duration models lies in the use of a categorical time variable (which is the time variable that defines the cross-classification and is D in the present example) versus interval-scale time covariates (which are DR, DR2, D0, LDR, and LDR2 in the present example) in specifying the main effects of duration. Note that all of the nonparametric duration models (lines 37-44) use D. The parameters for D characterize the baseline hazard function that is not restricted in form. In contrast, none of the parametric duration models (lines 21-35) uses D. Instead, time covariates are used in each model to parameterize a functionally specified form of duration dependence.

Goodness-of-Fit Tests and Comparisons of Models

Table 4.4 presents the results from the application of 22 models that are specified in the program given in Table 4.3. Remember that the relative goodness of fit should be compared between models that are nested and where one model fits the data.

Table 4.4 shows that no models that have a parametric characterization for duration dependence (i.e., Models 3 to 16) fit the data

Table 4.4

Analysis of Data in Table 4.2

Models	Likelihood-Ratio Chi-Square	df	P
I. Constant Rate Models			
(1) [Null Effect]	527.44	113	.000
(2) (F)	359.30	108	.000
II. Parametric Duration Models with Covariates DR and DR2 (=DR^2)			
(3) (DR)	370.35	112	.000
(4) (DR)(DR2)	363.39	111	.000
(5) (F)(DR)	246.47	107	.000
(6) (F)(DR)(DR2)	238.20	106	.000
(7) (F)(DR)(F*DR)	238.01	102	.000
(8) (F)(DR)(DR2)(F*DR)	230.87	101	.000
(9) (F)(DR)(DR2)(F*DR)(F*DR2)	216.69	96	.000
III. Parametric Duration Models Using Log-Duration (LDR) and LDR2 (=LDR^2) and a Dummy Variable for Period Zero (D0) as Covariates			
(10) (D0)(LDR)	370.00	111	.000
(11) (D0)(LDR)(LDR2)	271.74	110	.000
(12) (F)(D0)(LDR)	235.94	106	.000
(13) (F)(D0)(LDR)(LDR2)	149.10	105	.003
(14) (F)(D0)(LDR)(F*LDR)	219.54	101	.000
(15) (F)(D0)(LDR)(LDR2)(F*LDR)	137.47	100	.008
(16) (F)(D0)(LDR)(LDR2)(F*LDR)(F*LDR2)	136.00	95	.004
IV. Nonparametric Duration Models: Proportional Hazards Models			
(17) (D)	233.09	95	.000
(18) (F)(D)	111.24	90	.064
(18) vs. (17)	121.85	5	<.001
V. Nonparametric Duration Models: Nonproportional Hazards Models with Interactions Between F and Covariates DR and DR2			
(19) (F)(D)(F*DR)	104.53	85	.074
(20) (F)(D)(F*DR)(F*DR2)	93.87	80	.138
(19) vs. (18)	6.71	5	>.200
(20) vs. (18)	17.37	10	>.050; <.100
(20) vs. (19)	10.66	5	>.050; <.100
VI. Nonparametric Duration Models: Proportional Hazards Models with Interactions Between F and Covariates LDR and LDR2			
(21) (F)(D)(F*LDR)	99.53	85	.134
(22) (F)(D)(F*LDR)(F*LDR2)	98.23	80	.081
(21) vs. (18)	11.71	5	.050
(22) vs. (21)	1.30	5	.900

NOTE: F = firm size; D = duration (categorical); DR = linear effect of duration; DR2 = quadratic effect of duration; LDR = log-linear effect of duration; LDR2 = squared log-linear effect of duration; D0 = dummy covariate for the zero period.

well. On the other hand, the proportional hazards model with a non-parametric characterization for duration dependence (i.e., Model 18) fits the data to a reasonable extent ($p > .05$).

Four additional nonparametric duration models, Models 19-22, test whether specific characterizations for interaction effects of duration and firm size provide a further improvement in the fit of Model 18. Model 19, which adds to Model 18 the interaction effects of linear duration and firm size, does not improve the fit of Model 18 significantly ($p > .20$). Model 20, which introduces both the interactions of linear and quadratic terms of duration with firm size, attains marginal significance ($.05 < p < .10$) when compared with Model 18. This model shows the same level of improvement over Model 19, too. The choice between these models in terms of the relative goodness of fit is, therefore, somewhat ambiguous.

On the other hand, Model 21, which hypothesizes the interaction effects of log(duration) and firm size, excluding period zero, attains a significant level ($p < .05$) of improvement over Model 18. Model 22 adds to Model 21 the interaction effects of the square of log(duration) and firm size, but does not improve the fit of Model 21 ($p > .90$). Hence, among Models 18, 21 and 22, Model 21 clearly shows the most parsimonious fit.

Because of differences in the characterization of duration dependence, two sets of nonproportional hazards models, Models 19 and 20 in one group and Models 21 and 22 in the other, cannot be directly compared by the conditional likelihood test. However, as determined by an indirect comparison of the two sets of models with Model 18, Model 21 has attained the most parsimonious fit with the data.

Interpretation of Parameter Estimates

This section presents the interpretation of parameter estimates from Models 18 and 21. Although Model 21 obtains an improvement in fit relative to Model 18, an interpretation of Model 18 is provided because it is a proportional hazards model and provides the basis for other models that modify it. Table 4.5 presents the parameter estimates from Models 18 and 21. In Table 4.5, the estimates of lambda for the last category are also presented. They are calculated as the negative of the sum of all other lambda values of the same variable. Thus, while the estimates for 29 parameters are obtained from the output of the SPSS-LOGLINEAR program for Model 21, the estimates for 32

Table 4.5
Parameter Estimates from Models 18 and 21

Parameter Number	Category	Duration	Lambda Model 18 (in years)	Model 21	LDR
1	D-0	0	-0.436[**]	-0.434[*]	0.000[a]
2	D-1	1	0.416[***]	0.417[***]	0.000
3	D-2	2	0.670[***]	0.669[***]	0.693
4	D-3	3	0.799[***]	0.792[***]	1.099
5	D-4	4	0.676[***]	0.665[***]	1.386
6	D-5	5	0.778[***]	0.764[***]	1.609
7	D-6	6	0.367[**]	0.355[**]	1.792
8	D-7	7	0.323[*]	0.311[*]	1.946
9	D-8	8	0.140	0.129	2.079
10	D-9	9	-0.038	-0.046	2.197
11	D-10	10	0.466[**]	0.461[**]	2.303
12	D-11	11	-0.520[*]	-0.524[*]	2.398
13	D-12	12	0.079	0.075	2.485
14	D-13	13-14	-0.811[***]	-0.812[***]	2.603
15	D-14	15-16	-0.570[**]	-0.566[*]	2.741
16	D-15	17-18	-0.322	-0.322	2.862
17	D-16	19-22	-0.268	-0.261	3.020
18	D-17	23-26	-1.056[**]	-1.015[**]	3.199
	D-18	27-30	[-0.693][b]	[-0.658][b]	3.350
		Firm Size			
19	F-1	0-4	0.504[***]	0.140	
20	F-2	5-29	0.280[***]	0.224[*]	
21	F-3	3-299	0.031	0.027	
22	F-4	300-999	0.014	0.177	
24	F-5	1000+	-0.488[***]	-0.466[***]	
	F-6	Government	[-0.341][b]	[-0.102][b]	
25	(F-1)×LDR		—	0.285[**]	
26	(F-2)×LDR		—	0.038	
27	(F-3)×LDR		—	-0.002	
28	(F-4)×LDR		—	-0.130	
29	(F-5)×LDR		—	-0.019	
	(F-6)×LDR	-		[-0.172][b]	

a. Set at zero because the interaction does not involve this category. Other values of LDR are the ln(midpoint of duration).
b. Derived as the negative sum of all parameter estimates for the specified effect.
[*]$p < .05$; [**]$p < .01$; [***]$p < .001$.

lambda values are presented in the table by adding three estimates of lambda values for the last category.

Model 18

First, we interpret the parameters estimated by Model 18. Since Model 18 is a proportional hazards model without any interaction effects of duration and firm size, the estimates for duration parameters and those for firm size can be interpreted separately. The duration effects show that the log-rates of interfirm job mobility increase rather rapidly during the first three time periods, and then gradually decrease with some fluctuations. Sudden increases occur at the tenth and twelfth years. While the tenth-year increase may be related to the fact that some firms provide better retirement allowances to employees who work 10 years or more, the twelfth-year increase is rather unexpected. Log-rates of job mobility seem to peak around the third to the sixth years.

The firm-size effects indicate that the smallest group of firms (0-4 employees) has the highest rate of interfirm job mobility, followed by the second smallest group of firms (5-29 employees). The next two categories, firms with 30-299 employees and firms with 300-999 employees, have about the same level of interfirm job mobility. The last two categories (private firms with 1,000 or more employees and government agencies) have the smallest rates of interfirm job mobility. The rate of job mobility is 2.70 (= exp[.504 − (−.488)]) times higher for employees in the smallest firms compared with those in the largest private firms. These findings support Hypothesis 1.

Interested researchers can test whether the difference in the firm-size effects between any two categories is significant using the results from the variance-covariance matrix of parameter estimates. This procedure is described in Chapter 3.

Model 21

The interpretation of parameters from Model 21 is slightly more complicated because of the presence of the factor ($F \times LDR$) in the model.

The relative log-rates for cell (t, i), where $D = t$ and $F = i$, expected from this model are given by

$$[\text{main effects of D for } t] + [\text{main effect of F for } i] \\ + [(\text{effect for } F \times LDR) \times (\text{score for category } t)] \tag{4.7}$$

where in this model,

$$\text{score} = \begin{cases} \ln(\text{mid–point of category } t) & \text{for } t \geq 1 \\ 0 & \text{for } t = 0 \end{cases} \tag{4.8}$$

Table 4.6

Relative Log-Rates Expected from Model 21 by Duration and Firm
Size

Duration Category	Midpoint of Duration	Firm Size Category					
		1	*2*	*3*	*4*	*5*	*6*
0	0.25	-0.2940	-0.2100	-0.4077	-0.2576	-0.9008	-0.5366
1	1	0.5575	0.6414	0.4438	0.5938	-0.0494	0.3149
2	2	1.0067	0.9195	0.6942	0.7555	0.1892	0.4475
3	3	1.2458	1.0586	0.8171	0.8266	0.3051	0.5015
4	4	1.2000	0.9418	0.6888	0.6615	0.1719	0.3244
5	5	1.3629	1.0496	0.7877	0.7318	0.2669	0.3854
6	6	1.0056	0.6474	0.3782	0.2990	-0.1457	-0.0551
7	7	1.0059	0.6097	0.3343	0.2353	-0.1923	-0.1252
8	8	0.8613	0.4321	0.1514	0.0353	-0.3775	-0.3308
9	9	0.7204	0.2621	-0.0233	-0.1544	-0.5542	-0.5255
10	10	1.2576	0.7733	0.4837	0.3391	-0.0490	-0.0364
11	11	0.2995	-0.2083	-0.5017	-0.6585	-1.0361	-1.0380
12	12	0.9235	0.3942	0.0937	-0.0706	-0.4385	-0.4538
13	13.5	0.0701	-0.4882	-0.7898	-0.9728	-1.3277	-1.3609
14	15.5	0.3551	-0.2374	-0.5445	-0.7452	-1.0847	-1.1391
15	17.5	0.6335	0.0111	-0.3009	-0.5171	-0.8432	-0.9161
16	20.5	0.7400	0.0785	-0.2398	-0.4762	-0.7848	-0.8818
17	24.5	0.0360	-0.6695	-0.9948	-1.2541	-1.5430	-1.6672
18	28.5	0.4359	-0.3069	-0.6384	-0.9170	-1.1891	-1.3364

As in the general case, the calculation of the relative log-rates for
Model 21 excludes the constant parameter λ. It is quite useful to depict
the relative log-rates in a figure to see how the log-rates of having an
interfirm job separation change as a function of duration and firm
size. Table 4.6 provides the results for the relative log-rates and
Figure 4.2 depicts these numbers.

Note that Figure 4.2 is based on parameter estimates from Model
21, where the interaction between duration and firm size takes into
account only the interaction having a smooth change with time.
Hence the similar shapes of ups and downs in log-rates among firm-
size categories as a function of time is an artifact of this imposition of
the specific form of interactions.

The results of Table 4.6 and Figure 4.2 confirm Hypotheses 2 and 3
regarding the expected form of interaction effects of duration and
firm size on the log-rates of interfirm job separations. First, employees
in the smallest firms experience a much smaller decrease in hazard

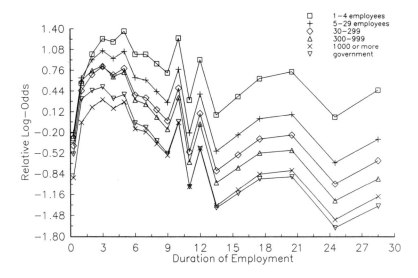

Figure 4.2. Interfirm Job Mobility

rates as duration increases. This finding is consistent with Hypothesis 2. Government employees initially have a higher rate of interfirm job mobility than employees in private firms with 1,000 or more employees. However, the hazard rate for government employees decreases as duration increases, and the reduction is faster than that found for employees in large private firms. As a consequence, for the period of 11 years and over, the rate among government employees becomes increasingly smaller than the rate for employees in the largest private firms. This finding supports Hypothesis 3.

The hazard rate for the second largest group of private firms, having 300-999 employees, starts rather high, but decreases faster than that for the largest private firms. In fact, the gap between the two hazard rates becomes smaller as duration increases. This suggests that as the duration of employment increases, job mobility among employees in firms with 300-999 employees will gradually acquire the characteristics of job mobility in an internal labor market (i.e., low interfirm mobility), whereas job mobility among employees in the largest private firms with 1,000 or more employees apparently has this characteristic from the beginning of employment.

CONCLUDING REMARKS

The illustrative analysis presented in this chapter employs a single time-independent variable, although the procedure can be easily generalized for the inclusion of additional time-independent variables. By including additional time-independent variables, various levels of interactions will need to be examined by following the procedure for log-linear analyses of higher-order tables (Fienberg, 1980). When the number of time parameters is large, the inclusion of interaction effects of time and other variables may create a large number of parameters to be estimated. The estimation for such a model may involve significant amounts of computation time and costs if the SPSS-LOGLINEAR program, or another log-linear program that employs Newton-Raphson algorithm, is used. The use of the SPSS-HILOGLINEAR program or any other log-linear program, such as ECTA, that employs iterative proportional fitting can provide a much more cost-effective calculation of chi-square values for those models, although parameter estimates are not provided.

Since the log-rate models are based on the use of cross-classified data, the analysis may appear to be limited as the data become sparse due to the inclusion of many explanatory variables, especially those that have numerous categories. Two considerations are relevant here, however. First, Haberman (1977) has shown that, with a small difference in the degrees of freedom, the likelihood-ratio test to compare nested models will still be effective if small cell frequencies are not due to a small sample size but to a large number of cells for a data set that has a sufficiently large sample size. Second, one can also use covariates to characterize the cross-classified data, without involving an additional dimension of cross-classification. Although covariates cannot characterize differences at the individual level, but can characterize differences only at the aggregate level of cross-classified data, their use will still provide insights regarding the effects of additional explanatory variables. (See Hout, 1984, for the use of such covariates for log-linear analysis of mobility data.)

Readers interested in a methodological foundation for the material presented in this chapter should refer to Holford (1980), Laird and Olivier (1981), and Schluchter and Jackson (1989). For log-rate models, see Haberman (1978, chap. 1), Clogg and Eliason (1987), and Agresti (1990, sec. 6.6).

PROBLEMS

(1) Using the data in Table 4.1, do the following:
   (a) Generate the data in Table 4.2.
   (b) Using the data in Table 4.2, generate the results of Table 4.4.
(2) Using the data in Table 4.7, answer the following questions (categories of occupations are defined in the notes to the table):
   (a) Calculate the sample survivors for each combination of duration and occupation.
   (b) Calculate the amount of exposure to risk for each combination of duration and occupation.
   (c) Using the SPSSX-LOGLINEAR program, test various proportional hazards models with the data. Employ models with both parametric and nonparametric characterizations for duration dependence. Identify the best-fitting model.
   (d) Using the model identified above, calculate the difference in log-rates for each pair of occupational categories, controlling for duration. Assess whether or not the differences are significant, given the 5% level.
   (e) Explore nonproportional hazards models. Confirm that a proportional hazards model fits the data more parsimoniously than any of the nonproportional hazards models that correspond to those tested in Table 4.4.

APPENDIX

This appendix presents proofs regarding the length of exposure to risk for the period zero, that is, the period in which subjects' ages are equal to their ages of employment.

We assume that entries into the risk period are uniformly distributed during the age of employment, and that the probability of having an interfirm job separation or censoring is uniform throughout the first year of employment. Let $a \geq 0$ be an arbitrary constant parameter for the assumed uniform distribution of the event or censoring during the first year of employment. It follows that $(1 - x)/a$ is the probability of having an event (or censoring) at the same age as the age of employment for persons who enter the risk set at time x ($0 < x < 1$) during the age of employment. As assumed above, x is uniformly distributed in the time interval $(0, 1)$.

Table 4.7

Number of Events and Censored Observations as a Function of Occupation and the Difference Between Age at the Occurrence of Interfirm Job Separation/Censoring and Age of Entry into the First Employment (nonfarm male employees aged 20-64 in 1975 in Japan)

diff.	Number of Events Occupation[a]						Number of Censored Observations Occupation[a]					
	1	2	3	4	5	6	1	2	3	4	5	6
0	2	2	8	13	6	3	2	7	0	1	1	0
1	12	27	21	43	33	17	3	4	3	1	0	0
2	13	33	20	48	44	15	4	10	1	4	0	1
3	13	28	28	49	36	14	3	13	2	5	6	1
4	4	24	16	48	28	6	5	10	4	4	3	2
5	6	27	15	33	31	9	4	4	5	4	8	0
6	6	10	13	26	12	4	1	7	1	4	3	2
7	6	13	5	22	8	3	7	8	7	7	7	2
8	7	7	8	9	9	2	7	10	5	6	4	4
9	5	6	1	9	5	4	6	9	2	8	3	1
10	3	9	5	15	9	5	2	17	4	4	3	2
11	1	3	3	5	4	1	0	12	2	1	6	0
12	2	7	2	7	5	1	2	8	2	4	1	1
13	0	1	1	2	5	0	3	10	2	5	1	0
14	0	3	0	1	4	0	2	10	2	5	3	0
15	0	3	4	3	0	1	9	6	1	2	4	1
16	2	2	2	0	1	1	1	7	2	5	2	0
17	1	2	2	3	2	1	2	5	4	3	2	1
18	1	3	1	2	0	1	4	7	1	2	3	0
19	1	1	1	5	1	3	2	9	0	3	4	3
20	1	1	1	3	1	0	2	3	0	3	4	0
21	0	1	0	0	1	2	1	4	0	2	2	0
22	1	1	0	2	0	1	4	4	2	3	1	2
23	0	0	0	0	0	0	3	4	1	2	1	0
24	1	1	0	0	2	0	4	6	1	1	3	0
25	0	1	0	1	1	0	3	2	0	1	2	2
26	0	0	0	0	0	1	2	8	0	2	1	0
27	0	1	0	0	0	0	2	3	0	2	1	1
28	0	2	0	0	0	0	0	4	0	0	2	1
29	0	1	0	0	0	0	0	0	0	2	0	1
30	0	2	0	0	0	0	2	2	0	0	0	1
							[8	17	1	17	5	5][b]

SOURCE: 1975 Social Stratification and Mobility Survey in Japan.

a. Occupation 1 = professional, managerial, administrative; 2 = clerical; 3 = sales; 4 = skilled; 5 = semiskilled; 6 = unskilled.

b. The number of cases censored because they have reached the upper limit of the 30-year duration period.

It follows that for those who have either an event or censoring before they become one year older, the average proportion of the year (age) passed before they enter the risk period is

$$\frac{\int_0^1 x[(1-x)/a]dx}{\int_0^1 (1-x)/a\ dx} = \frac{1}{3} \tag{A.1}$$

Since the event (or censoring) occurs uniformly during the risk period, the average amount of exposure to risk during the age in which employment started becomes $[1 - (1/3)]/2 = 1/3$ year, or 4 months.

It also follows that for those who survived until they became one year older, the calculation is as follows. The probability of surviving until the end of the period zero is $[1 - (1 - x)/a]$ for a person who enters the risk period at time x ($0 < x < 1$). Hence the average proportion of the year (age) passed before they enter the risk period is

$$\frac{\int_0^1 x[1-(1-x)/a]dx}{\int_0^1 [1-(1-x)/a]dx} = \frac{1}{2} + \frac{1}{(12a-6)} \tag{A.2}$$

Hence the average risk period during the age of employment is $(1/2) - 1/(12a - 6)$, where $a > 1$. Although this value varies from $1/2$ to $1/3$ as a function of a, it becomes close to $1/2$ if a is large. For the data in Table 4.1, the estimate for a, under the assumption that entries are uniformly distributed and the rates are constant for the first 12 months, is $S_0/[(N_0 + C_0)3/2] = 26.4$. Here $(N_0 + S_0)3/2$ is the estimate for the number of events and censoring for the first year if all subjects entered the risk period (i.e., employment) at the beginning of the age of employment instead of one third of a year after the beginning on the average (which is the empirical estimate). This estimate yields an expected length of risk period for censored cases of $12[0.5 - 1/(12 \times 26.4 - 6)] = 5.96$ months. Since this is close to 6, I simply used 6 months for the calculation of W_0 in Formula 4.6.

NOTES

1. If variable A has an interval scale, we may characterize the interaction between A and T in the form of uniform association. On the other hand, Formulas 4.3a and 4.3b can be described as row-effect association given that variable A represents the row. See

Goodman (1979) for the terminology. However, these uniform association and row-effect association models differ from usual log-linear association models because they are association models of log-rates.

2. In 1975, large private firms and government agencies in Japan had an early retirement policy, whereby many employees retired as early as age 55.

3. However, the likelihood-ratio tests between models with a small difference in the degrees of freedom will still be adequate for sparse data (due to many cells) if the sample size (i.e., total frequency) is large (see Haberman, 1977).

4. See Petersen (1991) for a more general discussion of time aggregation bias.

5

Continuous-Time Models with Cox's Method, I: Proportional Hazards Models, Nonproportional Hazards Models, and Stratified Models

METHODS AND MODELS

This chapter and the next mainly discuss continuous-time proportional hazards models and related models based on the use of Cox's (1972, 1975) *partial likelihood* (PL) method for parameter estimation. Continuous-time models based on maximum likelihood (ML) estimation are also discussed in this chapter, but no applications are presented. The emphasis on the use of PL estimation is in part due to the availability of computer programs in the standard statistical packages. Although several programs for continuous-time hazard-rate models with ML estimation are available, none of them have yet been included in standard statistical packages. Computer programs for the ML method are briefly discussed in this chapter.

Currently, the use of Cox's PL method is probably the most popular approach to event history analysis. This is especially true for demographic studies of marriage, childbirth, divorce, migration, job mobility, and the like (e.g., Carroll & Mayer, 1986; DiPrete, 1981; Fergusson, Horwood, & Shannon, 1984; Hogan & Kertzer, 1986; Lehrer, 1984; Michael & Tuma, 1985; Teachman & Heckert, 1985).

Continuous-time proportional hazards models based on the PL method have two significant advantages over continuous-time or discrete-time models based on the ML method. However, the use of PL method has some disadvantages as well.

The most significant advantage of the PL method is that models can assume time dependence without specifying its form. As we have seen in the examples presented in the preceding chapters, a parametric characterization for time dependence (or duration dependence) leads to a poor fit of the model with data in many cases. Hence it is reasonable to assume that time dependence can be more adequately characterized non-parametrically than by a specific function having a few parameters.

The second advantage of Cox's method is its ability to use strati-fied models, which are described later. A stratified model permits us to control for a categorical covariate (or a set of categorical covari-ates) that may have a complicated form of interaction effects with time, without specifying the form of the interaction effects. Stratified models may also be used for the analysis of repeatable events by specifying spells as strata (Blossfeld & Hamerle, 1989).

There are at least four distinct disadvantages in the use of Cox's method, although none of them is serious. However, the use of the PL method requires some qualification.

Cox's method uses only information about the relative order of dura-tion times, instead of information about the exact timing of events and censoring. Hence the loss of information can be great. It has been proven, however, that the PL estimators of parameters for propor-tional hazards and related models described in this chapter become asymptotically efficient under some regularity conditions (Efron, 1977; for related studies on efficiency of the PL estimators, see Oakes, 1977; Wong, 1986). Hence the relative lack of precision for the PL estimates of parameters compared with the ML estimates due to the loss of information is expected to decrease with an increase in the sample size for most empirical situations. However, the precision of the PL estimates of parameters can be much less than that for the ML estimates when the sample size is small. In fact, Coleman's (1981) comparison of the PL and ML methods suggests this situation. As an example in Chapter 6 shows, the alternative test statistics are sometimes not very close to each other even with a fairly large sample. Hence the PL method is not recommended when the sample size is very small.

The second disadvantage pertains to the presence of tied events, which was discussed in Chapter 2 in relation to the use of discrete-time models. The exact handling of ties in the PL method is com-putationally prohibitive and, therefore, the computer programs for the method employ a standard approximation. But the adequacy of the approximation has been called into question when there are many ties (Farewell & Prentice, 1980). Prentice and Farewell (1986) have stated, however, that "as a rule of thumb the bias is not likely to be severe if not more than 5% of the subjects 'at risk' fail at any specific failure time" (p. 14). If a serious problem of ties exists, the use of the ML method, especially with discrete-time models, is recommended.

Third, the PL method does not permit us to analyze the form of time dependence directly. If the form of time dependence itself is of substantive interest, the method is relatively disadvantageous.

Finally, the PL method is based on weaker theoretical foundations than is the ML method. Although the major asymptotic properties of parameter estimates are known, caveats are necessary for the procedure of model selection. This point is discussed further below.

In spite of all these disadvantages, Cox's method has been widely accepted and used in social science research. Its applications provide powerful analyses of event histories. At the same time, however, Cox's method has been used somewhat mechanically in social science research. Often a search is not made for a better specification of the hazard-rate model. In this chapter, I again emphasize the importance of model selection to attain a better-specified model. Specifically, this chapter discusses the test of nonproportionality and the modeling of nonproportional effects of covariates. In this connection, this chapter discusses two groups of models in addition to proportional hazards models: (a) nonproportional hazards models with a parametric characterization for the interaction effects of time and covariates, and (b) stratified models.

Two programs are available in the standard statistical packages for Cox's PL method, BMDP2L and SAS-PHGLM. While the BMDP program allows time-dependent covariates, the SAS program does not. Although the SAS program permits a test of nonproportionality with its BLOCK option, the BMDP program permits not only the test of nonproportionality with time-dependent covariates but also the estimation of the effects of any time-dependent covariates. Applications presented in this chapter and the next rely on the BMDP2L procedure in BMDP.

The use of time-dependent covariates is central in making a causal inference. A classification of time-dependent covariates and various caveats for interpreting their effects are discussed in the next chapter. In the illustrative application presented in this chapter, covariates are all time independent, except for the interaction effects of covariates and time, which by definition become time dependent.

Proportional Hazards Model

The proportional hazards model assumes that hazard rates are a log-linear function of parameters for the effects of covariates. Its value for person i at time t, denoted by $h_i(t)$, is given as

$$h_i(t) = h_0(t) \exp \left[\sum_k b_k X_{ik}(t) \right] \tag{5.1}$$

where $h_0(t)$, which represents the major dimension of time dependence, is called the *baseline hazard function*, and $X_{ik}(t)$, which may depend on time, is the value of the kth covariate for person i at time t. The baseline hazard function is common for all subjects. The model assumes that when X_k is an interval-scale variable, the hazard rate becomes $\exp(b_k)$ times as much for each unit increase in X_k, controlling for the effects of other covariates and time. If X_k is a dummy variable, the state with $X_k = 1$ has $\exp(b_k)$ times as much hazard rate compared with the hazard rate for the state with $X_k = 0$, controlling for the effects of other covariates and time.

If a functional form of the baseline hazard function, $h_0(t)$, is specified, the maximum likelihood estimation should be used. On the other hand, Cox's PL estimation permits the use of proportional hazards models without specifying the functional form of $h_0(t)$.

When covariates are all time independent in the proportional hazards model, the *survivor function* (or survival function), $S(t)$, which indicates the probability of not having an event up to time t, is given as

$$S_i(t) = S_0(t)^{\exp \left(\sum_k b_k X_{ik} \right)} \tag{5.2}$$

where $S_0(t)$ is the survivor function for subjects with $X_k = 0$, for $k = 1, \ldots, K$, and is given as

$$S_0(t) = \exp \left[- \int_0^t h_0(s) \, ds \right] \tag{5.3}$$

It follows that the *log minus log survivor function* is given as

$$\ln [-\ln S_i(t)] = \ln [-\ln S_0(t)] + \sum_k b_k X_{ik} \tag{5.4}$$

The first component on the right-hand side of Formula 5.4 is common for all subjects, and the second component does not depend on time. It follows that *if covariates are all time independent*, differences in the log minus log survivor function among groups with different covariate values become constant over time. This characteristic can be used in a visual examination of nonproportional effects for time-independent covariates, as discussed later.

Notes on Models Based on the Maximum Likelihood Method

Although this book does not present applications based on the ML method for continuous-time hazard-rate models, a brief discussion of some of the method's properties is in order. The ML method obtains the set of parameter estimates that maximizes the full likelihood function such that

$$FL = \prod_{i=1}^{I} h_i(t_i)^{\delta_i} S_i(t_i) = \prod_{i=1}^{I} h_i(t_i)^{\delta_i} \exp\left[-\int_0^{t_i} h_i(s)\,ds \right] \quad (5.5)$$

where $h_i(t)$ is the hazard function for person i, t_i is the time when either the event or censoring occurred for person i, δ_i is a dummy variable that takes 1 if person i had an event and 0 if the ith observation was censored, and $S_i(t_i)$ is the survivor function that indicates the probability that person i did not have an event from time 0 to time t_i.

The ML method requires a specification of the baseline hazard function. Several alternative parametric characterizations, including Gompertz and Weibull models, are possible (see Tuma & Hannan, 1984). Flinn and Heckman (1982) have introduced a general parametric formulation for time dependence that includes Gompertz and Weibull types as its special cases.

However, parametric expressions of time dependence do not fit the data well in many empirical studies of life events. Hence a parametric characterization of time dependence should not be used mechanically without testing its goodness of fit with the data. I recommend a step-functional approximation for time dependence, whereby (a) continuous time is partitioned into a set of time intervals and (b) time effects change only across the time intervals. Wu and Tuma (1990; see also Wu, 1989) also advocate the use of "local hazards models" that employ a similar semiparametric characterization for time dependence.[1]

There are several specialized computer programs that permit the use of continuous-time hazard-rate models based on the ML method. Tuma's (1979) RATE, Coleman's (1981) LONGIT, Yates's CTM (Continuous Time Models) (Yi, Walker, & Honore, 1986), Preston and Clarkson's (1983) SURVREG (Survival Regression), and my LEHA (Life Event History Analysis) (Kandel, Shaffran, & Yamaguchi, 1985) all permit the use of time-dependent covariates. (For some more alternatives and comparisons among programs, see Allison, 1984, app. C.) Tuma's RATE program has been used most frequently by sociologists, partly because of its early availability.

Yates's CTM program has incorporated some advanced features that are not available from others, such as Heckman and Singer's (1982) nonparametric technique for controlling unobserved heterogeneity.

In addition to these programs for modeling hazard rates, the SAS-LIFEREG program permits applications of some *accelerated failure-time models* for the analysis of censored duration data. These models are not discussed in this book.[2] See Lawless (1982) or Kalbfleisch and Prentice (1980) for accelerated failure-time models. The program for the generalized linear model, GLIM, can also be used for the application of various parametric models without time-dependent covariates (Arminger, 1984; Koch, Johnson, & Tolly, 1972).

Partial Likelihood Estimation

The PL estimates of parameters are obtained by maximizing the partial likelihood function. The PL function is given as follows: First, based on length of duration t_i, subjects are ordered from the smallest to the largest. The subscript i below indicates the ith subject after the ordering is made. Then the PL function is formulated such that

$$PL = \prod_{i=1}^{I} [h_i(t_i)/\sum_{j \geq i} h_j(t_i)]^{\delta_i} \qquad (5.6)$$

where $h_j(t_i)$ is the value of the hazard function for the jth subject at time t_i, where t_i is the time at which the ith subject had either the event or censoring; and δ_i is a dummy variable that takes 1 when the ith subject had an event and 0 if the ith observation was censored. The PL function is a product of *conditional* probabilities. Given that the event occurs at t_i, the ith conditional probability represents the likelihood that the event occurs for the particular subject who actually had the event at t_i rather than for any other subjects who were at risk. Since the PL function is affected only by the relative order of duration, information about the absolute timing of events and censoring is lost.

An important characteristic of the PL function is that when we insert $h_i(t)$ from Formula 5.1 into Formula 5.6, the baseline hazard function $h_0(t)$ is canceled out between the numerator and the denominator. Therefore, the PL function can be written solely as a function of parameters for covariates:

$$PL = \prod_{i=1}^{I} \left\{ \exp\left[\sum_k b_k X_{ik}(t_i)\right] / \sum_{j \geq i} \exp\left[\sum_k b_k X_{jk}(t_i)\right] \right\}^{\delta_i} \quad (5.7)$$

This implies that, although we assume the presence of a baseline hazard function that reflects the time dependence of hazard rates, we need not specify its functional form.

Modeling Interaction Effects of Covariates and Time, I: Parametric Models and the Test of Nonproportionality

Proportional hazards models assume no interaction effects of covariates with time. This assumption, however, needs to be tested empirically, and nonproportional effects of covariates should be included in the model if they are significant. The BMDP2L program permits us to test various forms of nonproportionality.

One way to test nonproportionality is to hypothesize a specific functional form of interaction effects between a covariate and time. If a significance test indicates that the interaction effects improve the fit of the model, then the hypothesis of proportionality should be rejected. Suppose we wish to test the possible nonproportional effect of covariate Z. The inclusion of $Z*TIME$ or $Z*LN(TIME)$ in the model, and a test of its significance, is the simplest way to test nonproportionality. The models can be written respectively as follows:

$$h(t) = h_0(t) \exp\left(\sum_k b_k X_k + c_0 Z + c_1 tZ \right) \quad (5.8)$$

$$h(t) = h_0(t) \exp\left\{ \sum_k b_k X_k + c_0 Z + c_1 [\ln(t)]Z \right\} \quad (5.9)$$

We can generalize the pattern of interactions by hypothesizing curvilinear time effects. For example, we can either add $Z*(TIME)^2$ to the model of Formula 5.8 or add $Z*[\ln(TIME)]^2$ to the model of Formula 5.9.

A more general way to test nonproportionality uses a discrete partitioning of continuous time. A set of time-varying dummy variables can be used to contrast distinct time segments against the baseline segment, and the interaction effects between a covariate and these dummy variables can be tested. This option does not strictly specify the functional form of the interaction effects. The model can be defined as

$$h(t) = h_0(t) \exp\left[\sum_k b_k X_k + c_0 Z + \sum_j c_j D_j(t) Z \right] \qquad (5.10)$$

where $D_j(t)$, $j = 1, \ldots, J$, is a set of dummy variables, each of which represents a distinct time segment against the baseline segment; c_0 represents the effect of Z during the baseline time segment; and $c_0 + c_j$ represents the effect of Z during the jth time segment.

The significance level for the test of nonproportionality can be assessed by chi-square tests, which are described in a later section.

Modeling Interaction Effects of
Covariates and Time, II: Stratified Models

Suppose that the interaction effects of a categorical covariate and time are so complicated in form that we cannot characterize them efficiently. Furthermore, suppose that we are not interested in the effects of this particular covariate and its interactions with time, but are interested only in the effects of other covariates. Then, we can make this categorical covariate a stratifying variable. The PL method for a stratified model permits the dependence of the unspecified baseline hazard function on strata (Kalbfleisch & Prentice, 1980). We can also use a set of categorical variables for stratification by redefining the combinations of their categories as values of a single categorical variable.

The stratified model is expressed for person i in stratum s as

$$h_i(t) = h_{0s}(t) \exp\left[\sum_k b_k X_{ik}(t) \right] \qquad (5.11)$$

where $h_{0s}(t)$ is the stratum-specific baseline hazard function. It follows that if we construct the PL function within each stratum, the stratum-specific baseline hazard function is eliminated from the likelihood function.

Although Formula 5.11 assumes that parameters b_k do not depend on strata, this restriction is not generally necessary. If all parameters depend on strata, we obtain parameter estimates by simply applying the PL method separately for each stratum. If some but not all b_k depend on strata, then we have a model that contains interaction effects of some covariates with the stratifying variable. Such a model, in principle, can be employed with the PL method. However, computer programs that are available in the standard statistical packages (e.g., BMDP2L and SAS-PHGLM) do not allow such models and assume that there are no interaction effects of covariates and the stratifying variable on hazard rates—that is, b_k, $k = 1, \ldots, K$—in Formula 5.11 do not depend on strata.

Let PL(s) denote the PL function for stratum s, $s = 1, \ldots, S$. Then the marginal partial likelihood function arising from strata $s = 1, \ldots, S$ can be expressed as

$$PL = \prod_{s=1}^{S} PL(s) \qquad (5.12)$$

The PL estimates of parameters for a stratified model can then be obtained by maximizing this marginal partial likelihood function.

The stratified analysis has both advantages and disadvantages compared with the analysis without stratification. The major advantage is that we need not specify the pattern of interaction effects between time and the stratifying variable. Another advantage in the stratified model is that we can plot the log minus log survivor function to examine visually the possible nonproportional effects of the categorical covariate that is used to stratify the data. The BMDP2L program can print the log minus log survivor functions for different strata in a single figure. An example is given later.

A major disadvantage exists in a stratified analysis, however. In formulating the PL function within each stratum, we can no longer compare relative duration times between observations in different strata. Accordingly, we lose information that could be obtained from the comparison. This additional loss of information leads to a greater loss of efficiency in the parameter estimation.[3]

Model Selection Under the PL Estimation

On the Use of Alternative Chi-Square Statistics

Model selection in the use of Cox's method requires clarification because the BMDP2L program, on which we base our analysis, gives somewhat misleading information for tests that pertain to the comparison of nested models.

Generally, we can obtain three different *chi-square tests* for comparing nested models under *ML* estimation: (a) the likelihood-ratio test, (b) the score test, and (c) the Wald test. The first one is described in Chapter 2; for technical aspects of the other two tests, see Rao (1973). The likelihood-ratio test has a significant practical advantage compared with the other two tests. Suppose that we have nested Models A, B, and C, where Model B is a special case of Model A, and Model C is a special case of Model B. If we get the likelihood-ratio test statistics for comparing Model A versus Model B and Model B versus Model C, the test statistic for comparison of A versus C simply becomes the sum of the two test statistics. This characteristic does not hold true for the Wald test and the score test.

Under somewhat different regularity conditions, all three tests are derived from consistency and asymptotic normality of parameter estimators. These conditions, which are met for the ML estimator, have also been proven for the PL estimator of the Cox regression models (Andersen & Gill, 1982; Liu & Crowley, 1978; Prentice & Self, 1983; Tsiatis, 1981). Hence we can expect all these tests should be valid with a sufficiently large sample under some regularity conditions. The manual for the BMDP2L program, however, recommends the use of the Wald test for comparing nested models. It gives the score and likelihood-ratio tests only as options because "the asymptotic distribution of the likelihood-ratio and the score function tests based upon the partial likelihood function have not been proved to be chi-square" (Dixon, 1985, p. 590). This statement is misleading because the Wald test does not seem to be particularly better than the other two tests.[4]

In practice, however, alternative test statistics often give quite different values, which apparently indicates the inefficiency of estimates for a given sample. Generally, since the PL estimation is not as efficient as the ML estimation, inconsistencies among the three test statistics occur more frequently. Hence I recommend *the use of more than one test statistic and a check of their congruence* to assess the reliability of the tests. The procedure is described in a later section.

Model Selection Under the Use of BMDP2L

The BMDP2L program provides several test statistics. First, it provides the "global chi-square" for each model. The global chi-square is the score test statistic.[5] This statistic tests the hypothesis that all parameters included in the model are zero. We can reject this hypothesis if the statistic exceeds the chi-square value for a given significance level and degrees of freedom. An important caveat in the use of the global chi-square is that *since it is the score test statistic and not the likelihood-ratio test statistic, one must not use differences in chi-square values to compare nested models.*

The likelihood-ratio test (or the Wald test) may be used in conjunction with the global chi-square for the significance test of all parameters in the model. In order to obtain the likelihood-ratio test (or the Wald test) statistic for this purpose, one needs to specify in BMDP2L a test that (a) uses the likelihood-ratio test (or the Wald test) as the test statistic and (b) eliminates all covariates from the model. The practical procedure of the test is described later in this chapter.

The BMDP2L program also provides three chi-square test statistics for comparisons of nested models using the TEST statements: the Wald test, the likelihood-ratio test, and the score test. The Wald test is the default test. The likelihood-ratio test or the score test can be obtained by specifying the appropriate options. Since the BMDP2L output includes the estimate of log-likelihood for each model, the likelihood-ratio test statistic for comparing nested models may be obtained simply as twice the difference in the estimated log-likelihood between the two models. However, the other two tests—the Wald test and score test—require a specification for the elimination of covariates whose parameters are hypothesized as zero.[6]

APPLICATION:
AN ANALYSIS OF JOB MOBILITY IN JAPAN

Data and Hypotheses

The application presented in this chapter uses data from the 1975 Social Stratification and Mobility Survey in Japan, which was used for the illustrative analysis in Chapter 4. It also focuses on the same topic: interfirm job mobility among male employees, where the dependent event is the first occurrence of interfirm job separation. For the same reasons provided in Chapter 4, employment durations greater than 30 years are treated as censored at the end of the thirtieth year. The example and exercise presented in Chapter 4 employed firm size and occupation, respectively, as the covariate of interfirm job mobility. The sets of categories for firm and occupation used in the following analysis are the same as in Chapter 4, and are also described later in Table 5.3.

The analysis in Chapter 4 is, however, limited in one major respect. It does not take into account possible historical changes in the patterns of interfirm mobility. Studies by Taira (1962) and Cole (1979) suggest that interfirm mobility decreased greatly in Japan from the time of the pre-World War II period to the time of postwar economic growth. The analysis presented in this chapter therefore focuses on the effects of three time-independent covariates: firm size, occupation, and age cohort. A trichotomous variable is introduced for age cohorts that, for 1975, distinguishes among (a) men aged 20-34, (b) men aged 35-49, and (c) men aged 50-64. This variable is not a time-varying age variable but a time-invariant variable for the distinction of the three cohorts. Four specific hypotheses are advanced with respect to these age cohorts.

Persons aged 20-34 in 1975 typically entered the labor force in the mid-1950s and later. The chaotic economic conditions of the post-World War II period were already stabilized by the mid-1950s, and there were considerably smaller rates of job turnover during the 1950s. A period of rapid economic growth started around 1960. Labor became consistently short in supply, thereby prompting employers to retain workers, especially those who had acquired a certain amount of tenure and job skills. Thus we can hypothesize:

- *Hypothesis 1:* The rate of interfirm mobility is lowest for the cohort with ages 20-34 in 1975.
- *Hypothesis 2:* The negative duration effect will be the strongest for this age cohort.

Persons aged 35-49 in 1975 typically entered the labor force during the war and in the early postwar period. To the extent that their labor force participation spanned the period of economic stabilization and subsequent economic growth, this cohort should also experience a decrease in the rate of interfirm mobility as tenure increases.

On the other hand, persons aged 50-64 in 1975 (who were 20-34 at the end of the war) typically entered the labor force in the prewar period. Careers for the majority of people in this cohort were disrupted by compulsory military service. Hence we can expect:

- *Hypothesis 3:* The rate of interfirm mobility is highest for the cohort with ages 50-64 in 1975.
- *Hypothesis 4:* The negative duration effect will be the smallest for this age cohort.

Hypotheses 1 and 3 can be tested by assessing the main effects of age cohorts on the rates of interfirm job mobility. Hypotheses 2 and 4 lead to a test of interaction effects of employment duration and age cohorts on the rates.

Programming of Models

The analysis presented in this chapter relies on the use of BMDP2L. A sample of the program is given in Table 5.1. Similar to the example used in Chapter 3, the BMDP2L program was called through SAS using the SAS BMDP procedure. The first three lines give the statements that are needed to use this procedure. (See Chapter 3 for explanation of these statements.)

Line 4, PRINT COV, is optional. The inclusion of this statement prints the variance-covariance matrix of parameter estimates.

Lines 5-9, a set of FORM statements, specify the characteristics of the dependent variable. Line 5, the UNIT statement, specifies the unit of measurement (year) for the duration variable. Line 6, the TIME statement, specifies the name of the duration variable. Variable DUR, which is in the input SAS data file JOBMOB, is specified here. Line 7, the STATUS statement, specifies the variable that distinguishes an occurrence of the event from censoring. The variable DC in the input data file represents the distinction here. Lines 8 and 9, as a pair, indicate values for the variable specified in the STATUS statement. When the event occurs, the variable takes the value specified in the RESP= statement, and when the observation is censored, the variable takes the value specified in the LOSS= statement. In fact, RESP=1 and LOSS=0 are defaults, so lines 8 and 9 can be omitted in the present case.

Lines 10 and 11, REGR (regression) statements, specify the covariates. Line 10, the COVA (covariates) statement, specifies the set of *time-independent* covariates that are included in the model. Covariates FS1-FS5 each contrast a distinct firm-size category against the baseline category, covariates OC1-OC5 each contrast a distinct occupational category against the baseline category, and covariates CHT1-CHT2 each contrast a distinct age cohort category against the baseline category.

Line 11, the ADD statement, specifies a set of *time-dependent* covariates that are included in the model. These covariates have to be defined by either a set of functions or a FORTRAN program. Since function statements are sufficiently flexible to define various time-dependent covariates, they are used exclusively in this book.

Table 5.1

A Sample Program for BMDP2L

	Line[a]
BMDP PROG=BMDP2L DATA=JOBMOB;	1
PARMCARDS;	2
/ INPUT UNIT=3. CODE="JOBMOB".	3
/ PRINT COV.	4
/ FORM UNIT=YEAR.	5
TIME=DUR.	6
STATUS=DC.	7
RESP=1.	8
LOSS=0.	9
/ REGR COVA=FS1, FS2, FS3, FS4, FS5, OC1, OC2, OC3, OC4, OC5, CHT1, CHT2.	10
ADD = INT1, INT2, INT3, INT4, INT5, INT6, INT7.	11
/ FUNC INT1=0.	12
INT2=0.	13
INT3=0.	14
INT4=0.	15
INT5=0.	16
INT6=0.	17
INT7=0.	18
IF (TIME NE 0) THEN INT1=FS1*LN(TIME).	19
IF (TIME NE 0) THEN INT2=FS2*LN(TIME).	20
IF (TIME NE 0) THEN INT3=FS3*LN(TIME).	21
IF (TIME NE 0) THEN INT4=FS4*LN(TIME).	22
IF (TIME NE 0) THEN INT5=FS5*LN(TIME).	23
IF (TIME NE 0) THEN INT6=CHT1*LN(TIME).	24
IF (TIME NE 0) THEN INT7=CHT2*LN(TIME).	25
/ TEST STAT=LRATIO.	26
ELIM=INT1, INT2, INT3, INT4, INT5.	27
ELIM=INT6, INT7.	28
ELIM=FS1, FS2, FS3, FS4, FS5, OC1, OC2, OC3, OC4, OC5, INT1, INT2, INT3, INT4, INT5, INT6, INT7.	29
/ END	30
/ FINISH	31
;	32

a. Line numbers do not appear in the program.

Seven variables for interaction effects, INT1-INT7, are specified as time-dependent covariates to be included in the model.

Lines 12-25, the FUNC (function) statements, define the time-dependent covariates. In the present application, we follow the same characterization that was employed in Chapter 4 for the interaction effects of duration and covariates. We use the Weibull-type characterization for the interaction effects by employing LN(TIME)×[Covariate]. In the function statements, the keyword TIME represents the time-varying values of duration. As in Chapter 4, we assign 0 for the interaction variables at TIME=0. Thus, in lines 19-25, covariates INT1-INT7 are defined only for TIME>0. Covariates INT1-INT5 represent the interaction effects of firm size and ln(duration), and covariates INT6-INT7 represent the interaction effects of age cohorts and ln(duration).

Lines 26-28, the set of TEST statements, provide test statistics for specific hypotheses regarding the absence of effects. The statement STAT=LRATIO specifies that the likelihood-ratio test should be used. If this statement is omitted, the Wald test is used by default. Line 27 specifies a test for the absence of the interaction effects of firm size and ln(duration), Line 28 specifies a test for the absence of the interaction effects of age cohort and ln(duration), and Line 29 specifies a test for the hypothesis that all parameters for covariates are zero.

Suppose that we wish, rather, to use age cohort as a stratifying variable and retain only occupation and firm size as covariates. Then the program in Table 5.1 needs to be modified in the following way: (a) Omit CHT1 and CHT2 from the covariates in line 10; (b) omit INT6 and INT7 from the ADD statement in line 11, and drop their definitions from the function statement (lines 17-18 and 24-25); and (c) add to the REGR statement an option that specifies STRATA=CHT, where CHT is a variable that takes distinct values, such as 1, 2 and 3, for the age cohorts.

Comparisons of Models

Table 5.2 presents the results for seven models, A1-A7, that include firm size (FS), occupation (OC), and cohort (CHT) as covariates; for three additional models, B1-B3, that include only firm size and cohort as covariates; and for three other models, C1-C3, that include firm size and occupation as covariates and use cohort as a stratifying variable. Comparisons between nested models are made using the Wald test and the likelihood-ratio test.

The two chi-square tests are highly congruent and comparisons among Models A1-A7 consistently indicate that, regardless of whether other interactions are excluded or included in the model, (a) the interaction

Table 5.2

Comparison of Selected Models

Models	Global χ^2	L^2	df	P	
(A) Nonstratified Models with FS, OC, CHT					
(1) Proportional Hazards Model: Model A1	169.49	172.37	12	.000	
(2) Model A1 + FS×LN(TIME)	185.16	182.26	17	.000	
(3) Model A1 + FS×LN(TIME) + FS×LN(TIME)^2	186.01	183.08	22	.000	
(4) Model A1 + OC×LN(TIME)	173.12	175.16	17	.000	
(5) Model A1 + CHT×LN(TIME)	191.87	193.62	14	.000	
(6) Model A1 + CHT×LN(TIME) + CHT×LN(TIME)^2	194.72	196.48	16	.000	
(7) Model A1 + FS×LN(TIME) + CHT×LN(TIME)	207.90	204.04	19	.000	
(B) Nonstratified Models with FS and CHT only					
(1) Proportional Hazards Model: Model B1	120.27	117.83	7	.000	
(2) Model B1 + CHT×LN(TIME)	141.37	138.12	9	.000	
(3) Model B1 + CHT×LN(TIME) + FS×LN(TIME)	158.25	149.93	14	.000	
(C) Stratified Models with FS and OC: Stratified by CHT					
(1) Proportional Hazards Model: Model C1	158.78	160.25	10	.000	
(2) Model C1 + FS×LN(TIME)	173.63	170.02	15	.000	
(3) Model C1 + OC×LN(TIME)	163.44	163.83	15	.000	

Comparison of Nested Models

	Wald Test	Likelihood-Ratio Test	df		
A2 vs. A1	9.95	9.89	5	>.050	<.100
A4 vs. A1	2.79	2.78	5	>.700	
A5 vs. A1	20.31	21.25	2	.000	
A3 vs. A2	0.83	0.82	5	>.900	
A6 vs. A5	2.88	2.85	2	>.200	
A7 vs. A2	20.82	21.78	2	.000	
A7 vs. A5	10.46	10.42	5	>.050	<.100
B2 vs. B1	19.42	20.96	2	.000	
B3 vs. B2	11.86	11.81	5	>.010	<.050
C2 vs. C1	9.81	9.77	5	>.050	<.100
C3 vs. C1	2.51	2.50	5	>.700	

effect of age-cohort and ln(duration) is significant and strong (A5 versus A1 and A7 versus A2), (b) the interaction effect of firm size and ln(duration) is marginal ($.05 < p < .10$) (A2 versus A1 and A7 versus A5), and (c) the interaction effect of occupation and ln(duration) is clearly insignificant (A4 versus A1). Furthermore, the interaction effect with squared ln(duration) is clearly insignificant for both age cohort and firm size (A3 versus A2 and A6 versus A5).

In comparing Models B2 and B3, the two chi-square tests consistently indicate that when occupation is omitted, the interaction effect of firm size and ln(duration) increases its level of significance ($p < .05$).

Compared with the results from Models A1-A7, the chi-square tests for comparing Models C1, C2, and C3, which have cohort as the stratifying variable, do not change the results for the pattern of effects of firm size and occupation significantly. The significance of the interaction effect for firm size and ln(duration) is marginal ($.05 < p < .10$) (C2 versus C1), while the interaction effect for occupation and ln(duration) is insignificant (C3 versus C1). We cannot test here whether the use of CHT as a stratifying variable significantly improves the goodness of fit of the model with the data because Models A1-A7 and Models C1-C3 are based on different likelihood functions.

Parameter estimates from seven selected models—A1, A5, A7, B2, B3, C1, and C2—are presented in Table 5.3. If we compare the results from Model A5 with Model C1, and Model A7 with Model C2, we find that the parameter estimates are quite similar. Here, Models A5 and A7 use parametric controls for the interaction effects of cohort and ln(duration). The corresponding models, C1 and C2, use cohort as a stratifying variable, thereby controlling for any possible form of interaction effects between cohort and duration. The similarities between the two sets of results indicate that the particular parametric characterization of the interaction effects employed in Models A5 and A7 does not distort the results significantly. It follows that we get more information from the nonstratified models without having a serious bias in parameter estimates.

Comparisons of Models A5 and A7 with Models B2 and B3, respectively, indicate that the main effects of firm size change rather greatly if we do not control for occupation. Without controlling for occupation, we tend to (a) underestimate the hazard rates of interfirm mobility for government employees relative to employees in the largest

Table 5.3

Parameter Estimates from Selected Models

Covariates	Nonstratified Models					Stratified Models	
	A1	A5	A7	B2	B3	C1	C2
(1) Firm size (versus 1000 or more)							
0-4	0.864***	0.782***	0.449*	0.961***	0.621**	0.775***	0.462*
5-29	0.601***	0.597***	0.539**	0.731***	0.670***	0.596***	0.538**
30-299	0.452***	0.450***	0.435*	0.502***	0.492**	0.449***	0.438*
300-999	0.449***	0.428***	0.589**	0.436***	0.637**	0.434***	0.581**
govern.	0.391**	0.404***	0.656**	0.145	0.420†	0.400**	0.664**
(2) Firm size × ln(duration) (versus 1000 or more)							
0-4	—	—	0.269†	—	0.272†	—	0.252†
5-29	—	—	0.045	—	0.047	—	0.047
30-299	—	—	0.011	—	0.009	—	0.008
300-999	—	—	-0.125	—	-0.153	—	-0.115
govern.	—	—	-0.183	—	-0.195	—	-0.191
(3) Occupation (versus semiskilled)							
P,M,A[a]	-0.674***	-0.688***	-0.672***	—	—	-0.681***	-0.666***
clerical	-0.585***	-0.587***	-0.580***	—	—	-0.584***	-0.577***
sales	-0.074	-0.065	-0.055	—	—	-0.061	-0.052
skilled	-0.106	-0.110	-0.116	—	—	-0.109	-0.113
unskilled	-0.074	-0.063	-0.056	—	—	-0.064	-0.056
(4) Age cohort (versus 20-34)							
35-49	-0.036	-0.317*	-0.311*	-0.337*	-0.330*	N/A	N/A
50-64	0.188*	-0.422**	-0.431**	-0.422**	-0.431**	N/A	N/A
(5) Age cohort × ln(duration) (versus 20-34)							
35-49	—	0.257**	0.254**	0.253**	0.249**	N/A	N/A
50-64	—	0.479***	0.490***	0.469***	0.480***	N/A	N/A

a. Professional, managerial and administrative.
†$p < .10$; *$p < .05$; **$p < .01$; ***$p < .001$.

private firms and (b) overestimate the hazard rates for employees in the smaller three categories of firms, especially firms with 0-30 employees, relative to employees in the largest private firms. The occupation effects indicate that the two high-status categories—(a) professionals, managers, and administrators, and (b) clerical workers—have lower hazard rates than the rest. Therefore, the under- and overestimations of firm-size effects due to no control for occupation indicate that, compared with large private firms, (a) government agencies have a larger proportion of these two occupational groups and (b) small private firms have a smaller proportion of these two groups.

Interpretation of Parameter Estimates

Below, interpretations of parameters are given for Models A1, A5, and A7 based on the results presented in Table 5.3. Although Model A1 is not one of the "best" models among the models that were tested, it is the proportional hazards model. It serves as a departure point for other models and is therefore of some substantive interest. The results from Model A5 are also supplemented with graphs obtained from Model C1.

Model A1

The results for Model A1 presented in Table 5.3 indicate that the effects of firm size on the hazard rate decrease as firm size increases. That is, the rate of interfirm mobility is larger among smaller firms. An exception is that the rate for government agencies falls in between the largest and second largest private firms.

The effects of occupation reveal that two groups of workers, professionals/managers/administrators and clerical workers, have significantly lower rates of interfirm mobility compared with workers in other occupations. For example, the hazard rate for leaving the employer is 0.51 [= exp(−.674)] times as much for professionals, managers, and administrators compared with semiskilled workers, and 0.55 (= exp[−.674 − (−.074)]) times as much compared with sales workers.[7] The cohort effects in Model A1 support the hypotheses only partially. Although the rate of interfirm mobility is highest for members of the oldest cohort (as expected from Hypothesis 3), there is no significant difference between the youngest and middle cohorts. This does not support Hypothesis 1. But Model A1 does not take into account the possible interaction effects of duration and age cohort. Hence hypothesis testing needs to be examined further by models that take the interaction effects into account. This is done below for Model A5.

Models A5 and C1

Model A5 adds to Model A1 the interaction effects of cohort and duration. Although the interaction effects are very strong, the patterns of occupation and firm-size effects do not change greatly compared with the results from Model A1.

Model A5 shows that the greatest difference in the interaction effects of age cohort and ln(duration) exists between the oldest cohort and the youngest cohort (i.e., the baseline category). The strong positive interaction effect indicates that hazard rate for the oldest cohort in-creases at a greater rate with duration, compared with the youngest cohort. Although Cox's model does not provide the main effects of duration, we know from the analysis in Chapter 4 that hazard rates of interfirm mobility decline with duration. Hence the interaction effect of age cohort and duration, in fact, indicates that negative duration dependence—that is, the tendency for hazard rates to become smaller with duration—is the smallest for the oldest cohort and the greatest for the youngest cohort. These findings support Hypotheses 2 and 4, described above.

Because of the presence of the interaction terms, the effects of age cohorts vary with time. Therefore, the reassessment of Hypotheses 1 and 3, which pertain to the main effects of cohort, needs to take the interaction effects into account. For Model A5, cohort effects that vary with duration can be calculated as

$$
\begin{array}{l}
\text{Age cohort, 20–34:} \\
\text{Age cohort, 35–54:} \\
\text{Age cohort, 55–64:}
\end{array}
\begin{pmatrix} 0.000 \\ -0.317 \\ -0.422 \end{pmatrix} + [\text{Score of ln(duration)}] \times \begin{pmatrix} 0.000 \\ 0.257 \\ 0.479 \end{pmatrix}
$$

where the left vector gives the Main effects and the right vector gives the Interaction effects.

$$(5.13)$$

The results of these calculations are presented in Table 5.4. Since the numbers in Table 5.4 indicate the effects of the two older cohorts against the youngest cohort at each year of duration, the numbers within each row (duration) should be compared across columns (co-horts). The results presented in Table 5.4 partially support Hypothesis 1, such that the youngest cohort has the lowest hazard rates after four or five years of duration, but not during the first few years. Similarly, Hypothesis 3 is partially supported, such that the oldest cohort has the highest hazard rates after three or four years of duration, but not during the first few years. These findings indicate that initial hazard rates are relatively high when hazard rates of interfirm mobility decrease more rapidly as duration of employment increases.

A visual examination of graphs obtained from Model C1 that use age cohorts as strata provides supplementary information about the interaction effects of age cohorts and duration of employment. Since the stratified model can reflect interaction effects between time and age cohort without specifying its form, Model C1 can be regarded as a generalization of Model A5. Using the PLOT statements, we can

Table 5.4

Relative Log-Rates Expected from Model A5 by Duration
and Age Cohort

Duration		Age Cohort Category		
Category	ln(DUR)	20-34	35-54	55-64
0	0.000[a]	0.000	-0.317	-0.422
1	0.000	0.000	-0.317	-0.422
2	0.693	0.000	-0.139	-0.090
3	1.099	0.000	-0.035	0.104
4	1.386	0.000	0.039	0.242
5	1.609	0.000	0.097	0.349
6	1.792	0.000	0.143	0.436
7	1.964	0.000	0.183	0.510
8	2.079	0.000	0.217	0.574
9	2.197	0.000	0.248	0.630
10	2.303	0.000	0.275	0.681
15	2.708	0.000	0.379	0.875
20	2.996	0.000	0.453	1.103
25	3.219	0.000	0.510	1.120
30	3.401	0.000	0.557	1.207

a. Set at zero by definition for Model A5.

obtain the graph of estimated survivor function and that of log minus
log survivor function for each stratum. The graphs, however, can be
generated only for models without time-dependent covariates. They
also require a specification of the values of time-independent covariates included in the model. The graphs presented as Figures 5.1 and
5.2 are generated by using the baseline categories of firm size (firms
with 1,000+ employees) and occupation (semiskilled).

Figure 5.1 presents the estimated survivor function. It shows that the
survivor function for the oldest cohort (50-64) decreases more rapidly
than that of the other two cohorts. Differences between the two cohorts
are small, but the youngest has a slightly higher survival probability after
about eight years of duration. The graph of the survivor function is useful for obtaining rough estimates of the absolute level of the estimated
survival probabilities. For example, at the fifteenth year of employment,
the estimated proportions of employees who stay in the same firm for the
oldest, the middle, and the youngest cohorts, represented by A, B, and C
in the graph, are about 32%, 42%, and 44%, respectively, given the
baseline categories of firm size and occupation.

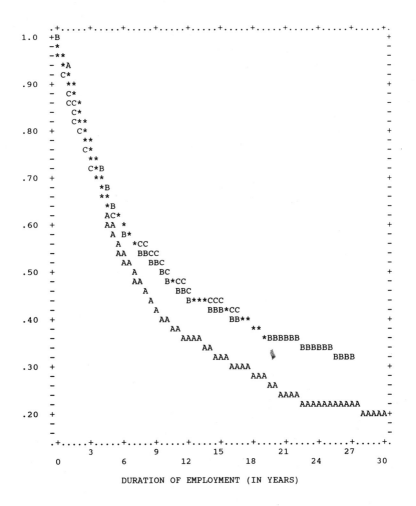

Figure 5.1. Estimated Survival Function from Model C1
NOTE: Age cohorts are as follows: A = 50-64; B = 35-39; C = 20-34; * = overlap.

Figure 5.2 presents the log minus log survivor function. If the co-hort effects are proportional, the graphs for different cohorts should look parallel. As we have seen in the results of Model A5, interactions effects between cohort and duration exist such that the older co-horts have initially lower hazard rates but have relatively higher

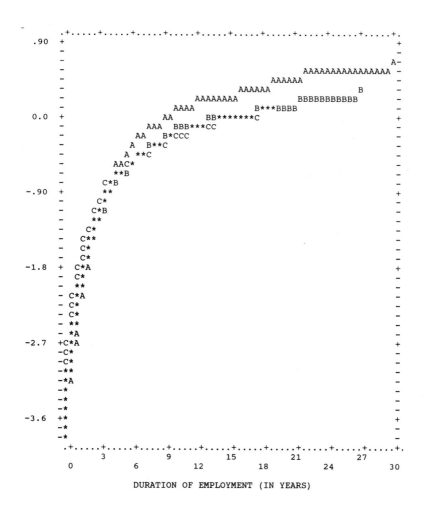

Figure 5.2. Log Minus Log Survival Function for Model C1
NOTE: Age cohorts are as follows: A = 50-64; B = 35-39; C = 20-34; * = overlap.

hazard rates as duration increases. Figure 5.2 confirms this: The oldest cohort (indicated by letter A) has a slightly lower log minus log survivor function when the duration of employment is short, but has the highest values as the duration increases. The opposite holds true for the youngest cohort (indicated by C).

Model A7

Model A7 adds to Model A5 the interaction effects of firm size and ln(duration). Because the occupation effects and cohort effects do not change greatly as a result of the inclusion of these interaction effects, only the effects of firm size are discussed below. The interaction effects imply that the effects of firm size vary with duration. Again, calculating the total firm-size effects requires us to take into account both the main effects and interaction effects. The formula for the calculation of the effects is the same as Formula 5.13, except that we have six categories for firm size and different sets of parameter estimates for the main effects and interaction effects. The results are given in Table 5.5.

Based on Model A7, Table 5.5 presents the effects of firm size on hazard rates of interfirm mobility as a function of employment duration. Since the effects at each year of duration use firms with 1,000 or more employees (category 5) as the baseline state, the data in Table 5.5 should be compared across columns (firm size) within each row (duration).

Table 5.5 shows that at the fourth year and after, the order of the relative (log) hazard rates among the six firm-size categories remains the same. The order is identical to that found in Model A1. However, the gap between the smallest category and others becomes increasingly larger as duration increases. The gap between the largest private firms (category 5) and the two next lowest hazard-rate groups—government (category 6) and private firms with 300-999 employees (category 4)—decreases as duration increases. These results are similar to those presented in Chapter 4, except for the following fact. In Chapter 4, after a certain duration, the hazard rates for government employees became smaller than those for private firms with 1,000 or more employees. This reversal in order does not occur in Table 5.5. The difference is due to the control for occupation. The results show that, controlling for occupation, employees in the largest private firms have consistently smaller rates of interfirm job mobility compared with government employees—though the gap between the two becomes increasingly smaller as duration increases.

CONCLUDING REMARKS

Cox's methods are described in more detail in many methodology textbooks, such as those by Coleman (1981), Cox and Oakes (1984),

Table 5.5

Relative Log-Rates Expected from Model A7 by Duration and Firm
Size

Duration Category	ln(DUR)	Firm Size Category					
		1	2	3	4	5	6
0	0.000[a]	0.449	0.539	0.435	0.589	0.000	0.656
1	0.000	0.449	0.539	0.435	0.589	0.000	0.656
2	0.693	0.635	0.570	0.443	0.502	0.000	0.529
3	1.099	0.745	0.588	0.447	0.452	0.000	0.454
4	1.386	0.822	0.601	0.450	0.416	0.000	0.402
5	1.609	0.882	0.611	0.453	0.388	0.000	0.361
6	1.792	0.931	0.620	0.455	0.365	0.000	0.328
7	1.964	0.972	0.627	0.456	0.346	0.000	0.300
8	2.079	1.008	0.633	0.458	0.329	0.000	0.275
9	2.197	1.040	0.638	0.459	0.314	0.000	0.254
10	2.303	1.068	0.643	0.460	0.301	0.000	0.235
11	2.398	1.094	0.647	0.461	0.289	0.000	0.217
12	2.485	1.117	0.651	0.462	0.278	0.000	0.201
13	2.565	1.139	0.654	0.463	0.268	0.000	0.187
14	2.639	1.159	0.658	0.464	0.259	0.000	0.173
15	2.708	1.177	0.661	0.465	0.250	0.000	0.160
16	2.773	1.195	0.664	0.465	0.242	0.000	0.149
17	2.833	1.211	0.666	0.466	0.235	0.000	0.138
18	2.890	1.227	0.669	0.467	0.228	0.000	0.127
19	2.944	1.241	0.671	0.467	0.221	0.000	0.117
20	2.996	1.255	0.674	0.468	0.215	0.000	0.108
22	3.091	1.280	0.678	0.469	0.203	0.000	0.090
24	3.178	1.304	0.682	0.470	0.192	0.000	0.074
26	3.258	1.325	0.686	0.471	0.182	0.000	0.060
28	3.332	1.345	0.689	0.472	0.172	0.000	0.046
30	3.401	1.364	0.692	0.472	0.164	0.000	0.034

a. Set at zero by definition for Model A7.

Kalbfleisch and Prentice (1980), Tuma and Hannan (1984),
Namboodiri and Suchindran (1987), and Blossfeld, Hamerle, and
Mayer (1989). The use of Cox's method in social science research is
by now abundant, especially in demography. For substantive applications of Cox's model, see DiPrete (1981) for unemployment, Carroll
and Mayer (1986) for job mobility, Hogan and Kertzer (1986) for migration, Michael and Tuma (1985) for marriage and parenthood,
Fergusson et al. (1984) for divorce, Teachman and Heckert (1985) for
first-birth timing, and Lehrer (1984) for birth spacing.

PROBLEMS

Table 5.6 presents a disaggregated version of the data analyzed in this chapter. The frequency data are cross-classified by duration of employment, age cohort, occupation (the distinction between non-manual and manual workers), and the status variable (event's occurrence versus censoring). Using the data, do the following exercises.

(1) Apply the proportional hazards model using the Cox method and the BMDP2L program. Interpret the parameter estimates for age cohort and occupation.

(2) Test the possible nonproportional effects of age cohort and occupation on hazard rates using ln(TIME)×[covariate] for TIME>0. Compare nested models with and without each interaction term using the likelihood-ratio test and the Wald test. Identify the model that fits the data most parsimoniously.

(3) Using the model with the main effects of age cohort and occupation and the interaction effects of ln(TIME) and age cohort, construct the table of relative log-rates by duration and age cohort. (Refer to the procedure employed in the construction of Table 5.4.)

(4) Apply the stratified model that uses age cohort as the stratifying variable and occupation as the covariate. Obtain the plots for both the estimated survivor function and the estimated log minus log survivor function separately for nonmanual and manual workers using 60 characters for the width of the plot size. Answer the following questions:

  (a) Does the effect of age cohort look proportional? Which figure(s) do you use for this examination?

  (b) For the oldest cohort, what are the approximate expected survival probabilities for nonmanual and manual workers at the sixth, twelfth, eighteenth, and twenty-fourth years?

(5) Apply the stratified model that uses occupation as the stratifying variable and two dummy variables for the categorical distinction of age cohorts as covariates. Obtain the plots for both the estimated survivor function and the estimated log minus log survivor function for the oldest cohort using 60 characters for the width of the plot size. Answer the following questions:

  (a) Does the effect of occupation look proportional?

  (b) What are the approximate expected survival probabilities for nonmanual and manual workers at the sixth, twelfth, eighteenth, and twenty-fourth years?

Table 5.6

Number of Events and Censored Observations as a Function of Occupation, Age Cohort, and Difference Between Age at the Occurrence of Interfirm Job Separation/Censoring and Age at Entry into the First Employment (nonfarm male employees aged 20-64 in 1975 in Japan)

| | Number of Events Age Cohort | | | | | | Number of Censored Observations Age Cohort | | | | | |
| | 20-34 Occu.[a] | | 35-49 Occu.[a] | | 50-64 Occu.[a] | | 20-34 Occu.[a] | | 35-49 Occu.[a] | | 50-64 Occu.[a] | |
Diff.	W	B	W	B	W	B	W	B	W	B	W	B
0	8	14	2	5	2	2	8	2	1	0	0	0
1	27	52	22	25	10	10	10	1	0	0	0	0
2	27	54	22	35	16	14	15	5	0	0	0	0
3	22	46	27	32	18	17	18	11	0	1	0	0
4	14	34	12	32	18	15	18	9	0	0	0	0
5	10	29	16	28	19	14	13	11	0	0	0	0
6	10	11	9	15	9	14	9	9	0	0	0	0
7	4	14	12	13	7	5	22	16	0	0	0	0
8	4	3	9	12	8	4	22	14	0	0	0	0
9	3	7	5	7	3	4	15	11	2	0	0	0
10	6	7	8	11	3	8	23	9	0	0	0	0
11	0	3	5	3	1	3	14	6	0	1	0	0
12	3	4	4	5	2	4	10	6	2	0	0	0
13	1	2	1	4	0	1	9	6	6	0	0	0
14	0	0	1	3	2	2	12	8	2	0	0	0
15	0	1	5	1	2	2	8	7	8	0	0	0
16	0	0	4	0	2	1	5	7	5	0	0	0
17	0	1	3	2	1	3	0	2	11	4	0	0
18	0	0	4	3	1	0	0	3	12	2	0	0
19	0	1	1	5	2	3	0	5	11	5	0	0
20	0	0	0	2	3	2	0	0	5	7	0	0
21	0	0	0	2	1	1	0	0	5	4	0	0
22	0	0	1	0	1	2	0	0	10	6	0	0
23	0	0	0	0	0	0	0	0	8	3	0	0
24	0	0	1	2	1	0	0	0	11	4	0	0
25	0	0	0	1	1	1	0	0	5	5	0	0
26	0	0	0	1	0	0	0	0	9	3	1	0
27	0	0	1	0	0	0	0	0	3	4	2	0
28	0	0	0	0	2	0	0	0	4	2	0	1
29	0	0	0	0	1	0	0	0	0	3	0	0
30	0	0	0	0	2	0	0	0	2	1	2	0
							[0	0	3	7	23	19][b]

SOURCE: 1975 Social Stratification and Mobility Survey in Japan.

a. W = white-collar work; B = blue-collar work.

b. The number of cases censored because they have reached the upper limit of the 30-year duration period.

(c) Are the results consistent between analyses 4b and 5b? If they are
not, what generated the differences? Which results are more reliable? (Hint: Which analysis takes into account the presence of interaction effects between time and age cohort adequately?)

NOTES

1. Rather than approximating the time dependence by a step function, they use a set
of smoothly connected time functions to maximize the local fit of the model with the
data in the neighborhood of each prespecified discrete time point.

2. Accelerated failure-time models are regression models for the logarithm of duration with censored observations. For the survivor function with parameter
$\theta = \exp(\Sigma_k b_k X_k)$, they assume $S(t; \theta) = S_0(\theta t)$. The models do not permit the use of
time-dependent covariates, and assume a zero limiting survival probability as time goes
to infinity. However, the assumption of zero limiting survival probability seems inadequate for many life events (Diekman & Mitter, 1983, 1984). A general class of models
that extends certain accelerated failure-time models to relax this assumption has been
proposed by Yamaguchi (1990a). These models employ a pair of regression equations,
one for the predictors of acceleration/deceleration of the timing of the event, and the
other for the predictors of high/low limiting survival probability.

3. For example, suppose we have $3N$ observations. Without stratification, we have
$3N(3N - 1)/2$ pairs of comparisons for the relative duration. If we distinguish three
strata of size N, the sum of pairs of within-stratum comparisons becomes $3N(N - 1)/2$.
In general, introducing M strata of about equal sample size makes the number of comparisons about $1/M$ times as many. The efficiency of parameter estimators decreases accordingly.

4. The score test should be a valid chi-square test because the asymptotic normality
of the partial derivatives of log-partial likelihood function and the consistency of the
Fisher information matrix (i.e., the covariance matrix of the partial derivatives of the
log-partial likelihood function) have been proven under some regularity conditions
(Prentice & Self, 1983). As for the likelihood-ratio test, it seems that no direct proof
has been given in the literature. In personal communication, however, Ross Prentice
stated that the choice between the Wald test and the likelihood-ratio test would make
no significant difference for applications of the PL method to exponential families, but
that the Wald test sometimes behaves oddly for models based on other distributions,
while the likelihood-ratio test does not. See Prentice and Farewell (1984) for a related
discussion.

5. The choice of the score test by BMDP2L for this purpose may be based on the
fact that when the PL estimation is used, the log-rank test provides a test of the hypothesis that all parameters in the proportional hazards model are zero. Under the absence
of ties in the occurrence of the event, the log-rank test becomes identical to the score
test. With ties, the score test statistic tends to be somewhat underestimated and, therefore, provides a conservative test of the hypothesis that all parameters are zero
(Kalbfleisch & Prentice, 1980, p. 81).

6. In comparing nested models, however, one model may not be directly obtained by
an elimination of certain covariates from the other model. For example, one model may

be obtained by imposing on the other model the identity of two or more parameters, such as $b_1 = b_2 = b_3$. A solution can usually be obtained by a reparameterization of models. Suppose we replace b_1, b_2, and b_3 with c_1, $c_1 + c_2$, and $c_1 + c_3$, respectively. Then the test $b_1 = b_2 = b_3$ becomes the test $c_2 = c_3 = 0$.

7. In the Japanese occupational classification, "sales workers" represent a more specific group than in the American classification: They are typically salesmen in retail stores, small real estate shops, and insurance agencies. This classification typically excludes those who work in bureaucracies, even if their primary work role is sales. Those workers are mostly classified as "clerical workers."

6

Continuous-Time Models with Cox's Method, II: Use of Time-Dependent Covariates and Related Issues

METHODS AND MODELS

The use of time-dependent covariates is an important feature of event history analysis. We are concerned with whether a change in the state of a covariate influences the hazard rate of having the dependent event. However, due to three major problems—unobserved heterogeneity, selection bias, and reverse causation—causal arguments that can be made are quite limited, as discussed in detail in this chapter. This chapter has two purposes. First, a classification of time-dependent covariates is presented, along with a discussion of different caveats that each group of time-dependent covariates requires for making a causal interpretation of their effects. In this connection, issues of unobserved heterogeneity and selection bias are discussed and methods for handling these issues are briefly described, although no application based on these methods is presented. The issue of reverse causation is also addressed. Second, a substantive application illustrates the use of various time-dependent covariates, with dropping out of college serving as the dependent variable.

Selection Bias and Unobserved Heterogeneity

In the observation of natural histories, people can self-select into different states of certain time-dependent covariates and/or differ with respect to the timing of entry into these states. Therefore, differences in the effects of these covariates on hazard rates, controlling for time, may reflect differences among groups of people found at different states of the covariates at each time, rather than the real effects of states on hazard rates. This is the nature of *selection bias* in time-dependent covariates. A randomization of people into different states will eliminate the initial selection bias, but this cannot be done for the analysis of natural histories.

Selection bias is also related to *unobserved heterogeneity*, or the issue of omitted variables, because the selection bias problem occurs when we fail to include in the model some "common antecedents" of the covariate and dependent processes—that is, variables that influence both the transition in and out of the covariate states and the hazard rate of the event under study.

When unobserved population heterogeneity exists, we either overestimate a negative duration effect or underestimate a positive duration effect (Flinn & Heckman, 1982). If the unobserved factor makes the hazard rate of having an event high for some persons, they will have the event and leave the risk set earlier, on average, than others, controlling for covariates that are included in the model. Therefore, the duration effect becomes confounded with the selection effect such that, controlling for covariates, the average hazard rate of having the event among persons who are at risk becomes smaller as duration increases. The bias in the duration effect will also lead to bias in the effects of covariates.[1] In summary, unobserved heterogeneity leads not only to (a) selection bias in the effects of certain time-dependent covariates due to uncontrolled common antecedents, but also to (b) bias in the duration effect due to an increasing proportion of subjects with relatively low risk in the risk set as duration increases.

Methods for Controlling Unobserved Heterogeneity

Several techniques to control for unobserved heterogeneity have been introduced in the literature. Two different groups of methods exist: *fixed-effect* methods, which assume a set of fixed person-specific effects, and *random-effect* methods, which introduce into the model a random error term (Chamberlain, 1979/1985; Yamaguchi, 1986). Fixed-effect methods can eliminate selection bias, but they can be applied only to the analysis of repeatable events and have other strong requirements for their applicability. Accordingly, these methods have serious limitations in use (Yamaguchi, 1986).

One type of fixed-effect method can be applied to the duration data from the *renewal process*[2] if we have at least two *completed spells*[3] (i.e., uncensored spells) from (almost) everybody in the sample. Here it is assumed that multiple spells for each subject are independent outcomes from the same proportional hazards model (or its extension) to which Cox's PL method can be applied. It is also assumed that although parameters for covariates are common among subjects, the *unspecified baseline hazard function differs among subjects*. It follows that the PL estimation for the stratified model can be applied by treating completed spells from each subject as independent observations of duration data and by *treating each subject as a distinct stratum* (Chamberlain, 1979/1985). This procedure uses only intraindividual, interspell comparisons of duration data for parameter estimation. If the data set contains only a pair of completed spells from each subject, and covariates vary only across spells, then we can simply use the logistic regression model by assigning 1 for the shorter spell and 0 for the other as the value of the dichotomous dependent variable. (For the analysis of paired failure data, see Kalbfleisch & Prentice, 1980, Section 8.1.) Time-independent covariates cannot be used with fixed-effect methods because their effects are "controlled out" as the effects of population heterogeneity.

Unlike fixed-effect methods, random-effect methods can be applied to the analysis of nonrepeatable as well as repeatable events and have fewer limitations in use. However, they cannot effectively eliminate selection bias because they normally assume the independence of the random error term from covariates that are included in the model. The random effect methods, however, can correct possible bias in the estimate of the duration effect.

Random-effect methods use a mixing distribution for the random error term. The mixing distribution specifies a functional form for the distribution of random errors in the population. Tuma (1978/1985) used the gamma distribution for this purpose. The gamma model can be applied in the RATE program (Tuma, 1979). However, Heckman and Singer (1982, 1984) have shown that parameter estimates depend rather heavily on the particular parametric mixing distribution that is used. They therefore advocate a nonparametric estimation of the mixing distribution. Heckman and Singer's model can be applied by using Yates's CTM program (Yi et al., 1986).

The issue of unobserved heterogeneity may be somewhat intimidating for users of event history analysis. Some users rely on computer programs that do not control for unobserved heterogeneity, while other users do not have confidence in understanding the sophisticated mathematics behind the techniques. However, the following advice is practical.

Bias due to uncontrolled heterogeneity is just one of many possible misspecifications of the model. There are many other ways in which a model can be misspecified.[4] For example, a model is misspecified if a significant interaction effect between covariates is not taken into account. Throughout this book, an emphasis is placed on searching for a better-specified model, regarding the effects of covariates that are included in the model. A careful modeling of the relationship between hazard rates and covariates can reduce the bias in parameter estimates substantially without involving sophisticated techniques (Clogg, 1986). Second, different types of time-dependent covariates require distinct caveats for the causal interpretation of their effects because covariates differ regarding the possible subjection of their effects to selection bias, unobserved heterogeneity, and reverse causation. By understanding distinct characteristics of time-dependent covariates, we can improve our analysis and achieve a better understanding of its limitations.

Reverse Causation

Another issue in the causal interpretations of time-dependent covariate effects is reverse causation. Below, the *dependent process* refers to the particular transition that is defined as the event of interest in hazard-rate models. A *covariate process* refers to the stochastic process that determines the value of a time-dependent covariate. *Reverse causation* refers to the influence of the dependent process on the covariate process. Reverse causation is an issue because the effects of a covariate on the hazard rate will be confounded with the effects of the dependent process on the values of the covariate.

In understanding distinct patterns of reverse causation, Tuma and Hannan's (1984) distinction between rate dependence and state dependence as distinct couplings of two interdependent processes is useful. Below, these terms are used to characterize two distinct forms of reverse causation. *State dependence* refers to a situation in which the covariate process is influenced only by the states of the dependent process. For example, if subjects' employment statuses are affected by their marital statuses, reverse causation due to state dependence is present when employment status is used as a covariate for the hazard rate of divorce.

On the other hand, *rate dependence* refers to a situation in which the covariate process is influenced directly by the hazard rate of the dependent event. For example, a psychological covariate, such as depression, in the analysis of divorce may be influenced directly by an increase/decrease in the hazard rate of becoming divorced.

The distinction between state dependence and rate dependence is used to classify time-dependent covariates below. This classification highlights caveats that are needed for the causal interpretation of covariate effects.

A Classification of Covariates and Limitations in the Causal Interpretation of Their Effects

Several different groups of time-dependent covariates are identified in the literature (Cox & Oakes, 1984; Kalbfleisch & Prentice, 1980; Tuma & Hannan, 1984). So far, there does not seem to be an agreement for the "best" classification. Below, several distinct groups of covariates are identified according to differences in the causal interpretations of their effects. The classification of covariates is mutually exclusive but is not exhaustive, and there will be covariates that do not belong to any of the following groups.

Time-Independent, Defined, and Ancillary Covariates: Covariates That Are Not Subject to Reverse Causation

Three distinct groups of covariates are not subject to reverse causation. One group is *time-independent* covariates, whose values do not change throughout the risk period(s) for each subject. Generally, two subgroups of time-independent covariate exist for subjects: (a) ascribed statuses that are constant throughout their lives, such as race and gender; and (b) statuses attained prior to (or at the time of) entry into the risk period (or prior to the *first* entry into the risk period in the case of a repeatable event) that remain constant thereafter. Examples of the latter are education at time of marriage and age at marriage in the analysis of divorce from the first marriage.

The effects of time-independent covariates are technically inseparable from unobserved population heterogeneity with fixed-effect methods. For the first group (i.e., ascribed statuses) it seems inadequate to make a causal argument for their effects, given that any causal argument is concerned with the consequences for a dependent variable due to changes in explanatory variables. Their effects indicate either that they are correlates of some unobserved factors that become real causes of changes in hazard rates or that groups are simply heterogeneous regarding the latent individual hazard rates.

Causal effects of covariates may exist for the second group (i.e., statuses attained prior to entry into the risk period). However, selection bias normally exists regarding the entry into different states of the covariates.

Two groups of time-dependent covariates—defined and ancillary covariates, according to Kalbfleisch and Prentice's (1980) terminology—are not subject to reverse causation, either. A time-dependent covariate is called *defined* if its total path is determined in advance for all subjects under study. A time-dependent covariate is called *ancillary* if it is the output of a stochastic process that is external to subjects under study. (For a more formal definition, see Kalbfleisch and Prentice, 1980, p. 123.) By definition, the values of these covariates are not influenced by the dependent process. The difference between the two is that while the values of defined covariates are predetermined even if they vary with time, the values of ancillary covariates are realized stochastically during the risk period.

Chapter 5 employed a covariate for the interaction effects of time (or ln(time)) and a time-independent covariate. This is a defined covariate because its value is predetermined for all subjects. Another group of defined covariates includes variables that become a fixed function of time for each subject, given their initial values at the subject's entry into the risk period. For example, individual age, historical period, and 12 months as a cycle, which are respectively employed in the analyses presented in Chapters 2, 3, and 6, are all defined covariates.

The effects of a defined covariate usually indicate the consequence of its association with factors that change the hazard rate, rather than that the covariate itself is a causal factor. For example, in Chapters 4 and 5, we found an interaction effect of ln(duration) and firm size on job mobility. The sharper decline in hazard rates as a function of employment tenure for government agencies, compared with private firms, may be explained by the government's wage structure, which gives a higher income return for tenure. If the government changes its wage structure, a possible real cause, then the pattern of the interaction effect will change.

Similarly, the monthly fluctuation of college dropout rates found in the application presented in this chapter seems mainly due to the combination of two facts: (a) Students tend to drop out at the end of the academic year and at the end of a quarter/semester more than at other times, and (b) colleges have certain months for the end of the academic year and the ends of quarters/semesters. If the majority of colleges systematically change their schedules for the academic year, then the monthly patterns of fluctuation in hazard rates for dropping out of college will change.

A defined covariate that is used for the duration of the risk period is subject to bias due to unobserved heterogeneity. For example, we normally observe a decline in the rate of *initiating* a particular deviant behavior, such as marijuana use, with age after a certain age, apparently because an increasingly high proportion of low-risk subjects remain in the risk set as age increases.

Selection bias may also confound the effects of a defined covariate when subjects' initial values of the covariate at the time of entry into the risk period are neither constant nor randomly distributed. One possible solution is a simultaneous control for the effect of a defined covariate that represents a time dimension and that of its initial value at the time of entry into the risk period. However, this solution usually leads to an identification problem, which is discussed in more detail in Chapter 7. For example, in the analysis of becoming remarried from the state of divorce, an attempt to separate the effect of time-varying age from the effect of age at divorce leads to an identification problem because the effects of age, age of divorce, and duration of the risk period (i.e., the duration of divorce) are collinear.

A genuinely ancillary covariate may be difficult to find in social science research because time-dependent covariates that are not defined are typically time-varying individual characteristics and are, therefore, not external to individuals under study. Time-dependent covariates that are approximately ancillary can be found among the variables that reflect changes in the characteristics of the population over time, provided that the sample size is negligibly small compared with the population. For example, in the analysis of the transition from employed to unemployed, a time-varying unemployment rate in the population that reflects changing labor market situations may be regarded as an ancillary covariate. While individual outcomes also contribute to the unemployment rate, their effects are negligible if the sample size is much smaller than the population size.

Selection bias may exist for the effect of an ancillary covariate. For example, regional unemployment rates or crime rates as time-dependent covariates will reflect the composition of the population of each region (i.e., selection bias). If the model fails to include the main categorical effects of regions to reflect their different initial hazard rates, the effects of regional unemployment rates will reflect differences in the composition of people among regions as well as the effects of change in regional employment or crime rates over time.

State-Dependent Covariates

As defined earlier, state dependence is a situation in which the covariate process is influenced by the states of the dependent process. Time-dependent covariates with state dependence will be referred to here as *state-dependent covariates.* The interpretation of the effects of state-dependent covariates requires caveats about reverse causation in addition to selection bias and unobserved heterogeneity. Caveats that are necessary for the interpretation also differ depending on whether the dependent event is repeatable or not.

Let's take an example in which the dependent event is becoming divorced from the first marriage (i.e., a nonrepeatable event), and assume that employment status is a state-dependent covariate. While the marital status of subjects does not change during the risk period of becoming divorced, the value of the covariate (employment) depends on whether subjects remain at risk (i.e., are married) or have already left the risk set (i.e., are divorced) at each moment. It follows that as the *duration* of the risk period (i.e., the duration of marriage) increases, the state-dependent covariate tends to obtain certain values more than other values. For example, being married, compared with being not married, may reduce the rate of having a job loss and increase the rate of getting a job after a job loss among men. Then, among male subjects who remain at risk for becoming divorced, we will find a smaller proportion of the unemployed as the duration of marriage increases. Hence reverse causation due to state dependence makes the duration of the risk period correlated with the states of state-dependent covariates. It follows that if the model we employ fails to characterize the duration effect on the hazard rate adequately, we shall obtain bias in the estimate not only for the duration effect but also for the effect of state-dependent covariates. The importance of modeling duration dependence adequately is highlighted by the fact that many time-dependent individual characteristics behave like state-dependent covariates.

A distinct issue of reverse causation may occur in the analysis of repeatable events. Since outcomes of the dependent process can affect the covariate process for a state-dependent covariate, the covariate state at the beginning of the second and later spells of the dependent process can contain information about the outcomes of the previous spells. Let's take an example of the hazard rate of becoming unemployed with marital status as a covariate. Since unemployment may promote the occurrence of a divorce, being divorced at the beginning of the second and later employment spells may contain information about previous employment histories. Generally, in the analysis of a repeatable event, the effect of a state-dependent covariate may in part be spurious because of its confounding effect with the previous outcomes of the dependent process, unless the latter effect is completely controlled for by other covariates.

In addition to these two problems of the reverse causation, the problem of unobserved heterogeneity, or omitted variables, is very common for models that employ a state-dependent covariate. Typically, some unobserved common antecedents of the covariate process and the dependent process can generate spurious effects of the covariate on the hazard rate.

Another potential problem arising from state dependence exists in sample selection. If the covariate and the dependent process are coupled by mutual state dependence, one should not select a sample based on a particular outcome of the covariate process because the outcome of the covariate process is not independent of the dependent process. For example, suppose we use only experienced labor force participants (i.e., persons who ever had a working experience) in the analysis of getting married. However, some people, especially some women, may not have work experience because (a) they married prior to getting jobs and (b) their marriages reduced the chances of their labor force participation. Hence, among people who marry prior to beginning to work, their inclusion/exclusion in a sample of experienced labor force participants depends in part on the consequence of marriage. However, a sampling that depends on the consequences of the dependent event (i.e., marriage) is inappropriate.[5]

Rate-Dependent Covariates

As defined earlier, rate dependence is a situation in which the covariate process depends directly on the rate of transitions for the dependent process. Covariates with rate dependence are referred to as *rate-dependent covariates*.

For example, measures of physical conditions among patients who are at immediate risk of dying are rate-dependent covariates because changes in the measures reflect changes in the hazard rate of dying.[6] Another example is an attitudinal/behavioral variable that reflects the effect of anticipatory socialization, which takes place prior to entry into a social role. Yamaguchi and Kandel (1985a) found that people tend to stop using marijuana during the year prior to getting married.

This apparently occurred because of the anticipated incompatibility of marijuana use and marriage. Thus marijuana use as a covariate for the hazard rate of getting married is rate dependent. An increase in the hazard rate of getting married changes the marijuana use state. Hence it is incorrect to conclude that stopping marijuana use increased the hazard rate of getting married.

Generally, if the rate-dependent covariate does not influence the hazard rate, but predicts it because the hazard rate for the dependent process affects the hazard rates for the covariate process, then the effect of this covariate is completely spurious and is a result of reverse causation. If the state of the rate-dependent covariate affects the hazard rate of the dependent process, we have simultaneous reciprocal causation. Generally, we cannot separate the causal effect of a rate-dependent covariate from the consequence of reverse causation in any simple way.[7]

However, a simple solution may exist in the case of anticipatory socialization. Assume that hazard rates of the dependent process influence the covariate process only during a certain fixed period prior to the occurrence of the dependent event. For example, assume that the anticipation of getting married affects certain behaviors within the year prior to marriage. Then, if we take a one-year time lag in the measurement of the time-varying behavioral covariate in predicting hazard rates of getting married, we can eliminate the effect of reverse causation. Although we usually do not know beforehand the exact period during which anticipatory socialization takes place, an analysis of the covariate process can inform us if any regularity exists regarding the time lag between a change in the covariate state and the occurrence of the event.

APPLICATION: AN ANALYSIS OF DROPPING OUT OF FOUR-YEAR COLLEGE

Data and Covariates

The analysis presented in this chapter is based on data from a specific subsample of the 1980 High School & Beyond survey and its two follow-ups in 1982 and 1984. The major outcomes from this survey were published by Coleman and his colleagues (Coleman & Hoffer, 1987; Coleman, Hoffer, & Kilgore, 1982). The sample employed here is made up of persons who (a) were high school seniors in 1980 and attended schools in the Pacific Basin area, and (b) entered four-year colleges when they first entered college. The sample is restricted to the Pacific Basin area to make the sample size small, so that the raw data can be presented here.

The dependent event is dropping out of college. Those who entered a two-year program are excluded from the analysis because leaving college with a two-year degree can be treated as neither dropping out nor the equivalent of graduating with a four-year degree. Hence the sample includes persons who initially aimed at attaining four-year degrees, and the dependent event is defined as leaving the college entered without the attainment of a four-year degree. For the majority of subjects, the period up to the second follow-up, 1980-1984, covers the major portion of the risk period for dropping out of college.

Censored observations are defined as either graduating from a four-year college or being in the same school at the time of the second follow-up in 1984. However, a small number of cases that are classified as dropouts from college may include students who transferred to other colleges. Although a college transfer is not a dropout, the two events share a common characteristic with regard to the student's original plan. It is assumed that subjects who entered a four-year college aimed at attaining a four-year degree there. Students who transferred or dropped out did not achieve this goal.

Four time-independent and three time-dependent covariates are employed in the analysis.[8] The time-independent covariates are (a) gender, (b) high school grades, (c) whether or not the individual entered college as a part-time or full-time student, and (d) the time lag between entry into college and graduation from high school. The time-dependent covariates are (a) ever married or not, (b) having a job with 20 or more hours of work per week, and (c) a set of 11 dummy variables for months of the calendar year. We may consider the first two time-dependent covariates as state-dependent covariates, and the third as a defined covariate.

The sample contains 265 subjects, including 107 dropouts and 158 students with censored observations. The raw data of the 265 cases are given at the end of the chapter, in Table 6.6. Variables that are used to construct the time-varying employment-status covariate (having a job 20 or more hours a week) are excluded from Table 6.6.

The categories and values of covariates are summarized in Table 6.1, which also presents a grouped distribution of the events

Table 6.1

Descriptions of the Dependent Variable and Covariates

Label	Value and Description	Frequency[a]	Mean[b]
I. Dependent Variable			
DUR(EVT=1)	event by duration		
	1-6	34	
	7-12	26	
	13-24	23	
	25-36	18	
	37-48	6	
DUR(EVT=0)	censoring by duration		
	1-24	0	
	25-36	4	
	37-48	154	
II. Time-Independent Covariates			
SEX	gender		0.570
	0 males	114	
	1 females	151	
GRD	self-reported high school grades		2.200
	1 mostly As	88	
	2 about half As and half Bs	83	
	3 mostly Bs	55	
	4 about half Bs and half Cs	31	
	5 mostly Cs	8	
	6,7,8 (half Cs and half Ds or below)	0	
PRT	part-time student		0.906
	0 full-time	25	
	1 part-time	240	
LAG	time lag between entry into college and high school graduation, range = 0-43		3.453
III. Time-Dependent Covariates			
MS	ever married		
	0 never married		
	1 ever married		
	(reference: ever married in the sample = 10.6%)		
EMP	employment		
	0 not employed or employed less than 20 hours per week		
	1 employed 20 hours or more per week		
	(reference: ever employed 20 hours or more per week in the sample = 58.1%)		
M1-M5,	monthly dummy variables; each takes 1 against		
M7-M12	June, the baseline month		

a. The data are not presented for time-dependent covariates.
b. The data are presented only for time-independent covariates.

and censored observations aggregated across months. In the analysis, however, duration is measured in months.

Substantive Hypotheses

The hypotheses postulated here are rather intuitive and are not elaborated. Other things being equal, I hypothesize that (a) better academic performance in school reduces the hazard rate of dropping out, (b) continuity of education reduces the hazard rate, and (c) the presence of role conflicts with schooling increases the hazard rate. High school grade is used as an indicator for academic performance to test the first general hypothesis; the time lag between high school graduation and college entrance is used to test the second; and marriage, time-demanding employment, and entering college as a part-time student, assuming that part-time schooling reflects the presence of roles that conflict with full-time schooling, are all used to test the third general hypothesis. No hypothesis is made for the effect of gender.

Programming of Models with Time-Dependent Covariates

In this chapter BMDP2L is again employed for the analysis, using the BMDP procedure in SAS. The time-dependent covariates that were employed in Chapter 5 represent interaction effects of time-independent covariates and a defined function of time. In contrast, the time-dependent covariates that are employed in this chapter are defined according to *auxiliary variables* given in the input data file, as described later.

Table 6.2 presents a sample program. In lines 3-8, pairwise interactions of time-independent covariates are defined in the SAS data step. Lines 11-12 indicate that the TIME variable, DUR, represents the number of months in college. Lines 13-16 indicate that the STATUS variable, EVT, takes 1 for dropping out of college and 0 for censored observations.

A set of regression statements appears in lines 17-22. In line 17, four variables (SEX, GRD, PRT, and LAG) and six interactions between them are specified as time-independent covariates in the COV= statement. Line 18, the ADD= statement, indicates that five time-dependent variables will be used in the analysis. In lines 20-22, auxiliary variables are specified by the AUX= statement. The auxiliary variables are stored in the input data file, HSAB.SASFILE, and are used in the function statement to define time-dependent covariates. The auxiliary variables themselves are not included in the model.

Table 6.2

Sample Program 1

	Line[a]
DATA RATEIN;	1
SET HSAB.SASFILE;	2
INT1=SEX*GRD;	3
INT2=SEX*LAG;	4
INT3=SEX*PRT;	5
INT4=GRD*LAG;	6
INT5=GRD*PRT;	7
INT6=LAG*PRT;	8
PROC BMDP PROG=BMDP2L DATA=RATEIN;	9
PARMCARDS;	10
/ INPUT UNIT=3. CODE='RATEIN'.	11
/ FORM UNIT=MONTH.	12
TIME=DUR.	13
STATUS=EVT.	14
RESP=1.	15
LOSS=0.	16
/ REGR COV=SEX, GRD, PRT, LAG, INT1, INT2, INT3, INT4,	17
INT5, INT6.	18
ADD=MS, EMP, INT7, INT8, INT9.	19
AUX=MRG, STM, JS1, JS2, JS3, JS4, JS5, JS6, JS7, JS8, JS9,	20
JE1, JE2, JE3, JE4, JE5, JE6, JE7, JE8, JE9, J1, J2,	21
J3, J4, J5, J6, J7, J8, J9.	22
/ FUN MS=0.	23
TM=TIME+STM-MRG.	24
IF (TM GE 0) THEN MS=1.	25
EMP=0.	26
TM=TIME+STM-JS1.	27
IF (TM GE 0 AND J1 EQ 2) THEN EMP=1.	28
TM=TIME+STM-JE1.	29
IF (TM GE 0 AND J1 EQ 2) THEN EMP=0.	30
TM=TIME+STM-JS2.	31
IF (TM GE 0 AND J2 EQ 2) THEM EMP=1.	32
TM=TIME+STM-JE2.	33
IF (TM GE 0 AND J2 EQ 2) THEN EMP=0.	34
....	..
....	..
TM=TIME+STM-JS9.	59
IF (TM GE 0 AND J9 EQ 2) THEN EMP=1.	60
TM=TIME+STM-JE9.	61
IF (TM GE 0 AND J9 EQ 2) THEN EMP=0.	62
INT7=SEX*MS.	63
D2=0.	64
D3=0.	65

Continued

Table 6.2, Continued

	$Line^a$
IF (TIME GE 12 AND TIME LE 23) D2=1.	66
IF (TIME GE 24) D3=1.	67
INT8=GRD*D2.	68
INT9=GRD*D3.	69
/ STEP = MPLR.	70
START = IN, IN, IN, IN, OUT, OUT, OUT, OUT, OUT, OUT,	71
IN, IN, OUT, OUT, OUT.	72
MOVE=0,0,0,0,2,2,2,2,2,2,0,0,2,2,2.	73
/ END	74
/ FINISH	75
;	76

a. Line numbers do not appear in the program.

The set of function statements given in lines 23-69 consists of three parts. The first part (lines 23-25) defines a time-dependent variable, labeled MS, for ever married. Two auxiliary variables, STM and MRG, are used here: STM indicates the starting year-month of college for each subject using a sequential year-month code that is defined as 12(YEAR-1980)+MONTH, and MRG, which is evaluated by the same year-month code, indicates the year-month of marriage. If the subject has never been married, MRG is set at 99.

In line 24, a time-varying variable TM is defined as TIME+STM−MRG. Recall that TIME is a BMDP2L keyword used to represent *time-varying* values of the duration of the risk period. The difference between STM and MRG indicates the time lag between the timing of college entry and the timing of marriage. If marriage preceded entry into college, the value for STM−MRG is nonnegative. It follows that TM is always nonnegative because TIME≥0 and STM−MRG≥0. For those who married after entry into college, the value for STM−MRG is negative. However, TM becomes zero when TIME+STM reaches the year-month of marriage (MRG), and becomes positive after that. If the subject is never married, TM=TIME+STM−MRG is always negative since MRG=99 and TIME+STM cannot exceed 99 during the observation period. It follows that since MS is initialized at zero (line 23) and becomes 1 when TM≥0 (line 25), MS represents the time-varying dummy variable for ever married versus never married.

The second part of the function statements appear in lines 26-62, where a time-dependent covariate for employment with 20 or more hours of work per week is defined. A complication here is that we do not simply distinguish whether subject ever worked or never worked. Rather, employment is treated as a time-varying state that may change several times during the period of risk. In fact, there are at most nine job spells per subject. The variable EMP is defined as follows.

Auxiliary covariates JS1-JS9 represent the years-months of starting the first to the ninth jobs, respectively. Code 99 is assigned for JS{i} if a subject does not have an ith job spell. Similarly, auxiliary covariates J1E-J9E represent the ending years-months of the first to the ninth job spells, respectively. Again code 99 is assigned to cases for which a spell does not exist. If the spell is censored by the survey, the auxiliary variables take the code for the last year-month of observation.

Another complication is that job spells for each subject may be overlapping. From the construction of the original job start variables, JS1-JS9, a later spell never starts earlier than a preceding job spell, that is, JS1 ≤ JS2 . . . ≤ JS9 hold true. However, a later spell can end earlier. This lack of ordering among the ending year-months of spells makes the definition of the variable EMP complicated. Hence the ending year-month variables were recoded in the SAS data set to satisfy JE1 ≤ JE2 . . . ≤ JE9. JE{$i + 1$} was recoded to be equal to JE{i} if the original order was JE{$i + 1$} < JE{i}.

The last set of auxiliary covariates, J1-J9, represents categories for hours of work for each job spell. The variables take the value of 2 for a job with 20 or more hours of work per week, a value of 1 for a job with fewer than 20 hours of work per week, and a value of 0 for the absence of a job spell.

Thus in lines 26-28 EMP is set at 1 when the subject enters the first job and works 20 or more hours per week at the job. Lines 29-30 recode EMP to 0 when the subject leaves this job. This procedure is repeated for the nine job spells (lines 31-62). Unless JE1-JE9 are recoded to satisfy JE1 ≤ JE2 . . . ≤ JE9, this definition of EMP may become inadequate.

The third part of the function statement (lines 63-69) defines other time-dependent covariates. Line 63 specifies the covariate for the interaction effect of MS and SEX. Lines 64-69 specifies two covariates, INT8 and INT9, for the interaction of GRD and a trichotomous time variable. Here the dummy variables D2 and D3 contrast the second year and the combination of the third and fourth years against the first year, respectively. These interaction terms differ from those defined in the SAS data step (lines 3-8) in that one of the constituent variables is time dependent.

The STEP statement in line 70 indicates that the stepwise regression of multiple factors, which are based on the likelihood-ratio tests, should be conducted. The next two lines specify that all main effects are initially included in the model (IN) and all interaction effects are initially excluded (OUT). Line 73 specifies that the main effects should always be in the model (number of moves = 0) and each interaction effect can move in and out of the model no more than twice. The order of covariates in lines 71-73 corresponds with the order in the COV and ADD statements (lines 17-19).

Table 6.3 presents an additional example of a BMDP2L program that uses time-dependent covariates. The program in Table 6.3 was in fact used to obtain the results of Model 5, which are presented later.

In Table 6.3, time-varying month variables are defined as time-dependent covariates. Their definitions appear in the function statement in lines 15-40. The auxiliary variables STM, starting month-year of college, takes 1 for January 1980 and increases by 1 for each subsequent month. Thus the current month of observation (MNTH) is defined according to duration in college (TIME) and the month-year of entry into college (STM) by subtracting a multiple of 12 from the sum of the two (TIME+STM) (lines 15-18). The variable MNTH thus represents months of the calendar year except that the value 0 corresponds to December. The procedure for defining a set of 11 dummy month variables M1-M5 and M7-M12, using June as the contrast state, appears in lines 19-40.

Tests and Comparisons of Models

Table 6.4 presents the results from five selected models. Many more models were tested using the stepwise regression procedure. For example, Model 1 was obtained by examining all six interaction effects among the four covariates in the model. Only the interaction effect of PRT and LAG was significant. Similarly, Model 2 was obtained after testing all possible interactions between the two time-dependent covariates, MS and EMP, and other covariates. Furthermore, for all covariates two tests of nonproportionality were conducted by hypothesizing (a) the interaction effect of the covariate and linear time (TIME) and (b) the interaction effect of the covariate and the two dummy variables that respectively contrast the second year and the combination of the third and fourth years against the first

Table 6.3
Sample Program 2

	Line[a]
DATA RATEIN;	1
SET HSAB.SASFILE;	2
PROC BMDP PROG=BMDP2L DATA=RATEIN;	3
PARMCARDS;	4
/ INPUT UNIT=3. CODE='RATEIN'.	5
/ FORM UNIT=MONTH.	6
TIME=DUR.	7
STATUS=EVT.	8
/ REGR COV=SEX, GRD, PRT, LAG.	9
ADD=MS, M1, M2, M3, M4, M5, M7, M8, M9, M10, M11, M12.	10
AUX=MRG, STM.	11
/ FUN MS=0.	12
TM=TIME+STM-MRG.	13
IF (TM GE 0) THEN MS=1.	14
PERI=TIME+STM.	15
X=PERI/12.	16
IX=INT(X).	17
MNTH=PERI-12*IX	18
M1=0.	19
M2=0.	20
M3=0.	21
M4=0.	22
M5=0.	23
M7=0.	24
M8=0.	25
M9=0.	26
M10=0.	27
M11=0.	28
M12=0.	29
IF (MNTH EQ 1) THEN M1=1.	30
IF (MNTH EQ 2) THEN M2=1.	31
IF (MNTH EQ 3) THEN M3=1.	32
IF (MNTH EQ 4) THEN M4=1.	33
IF (MNTH EQ 5) THEN M5=1.	34
IF (MNTH EQ 7) THEN M7=1.	35
IF (MNTH EQ 8) THEN M8=1.	36
IF (MNTH EQ 9) THEN M9=1.	37
IF (MNTH EQ 10) THEN M10=1.	38
IF (MNTH EQ 11) THEN M11=1.	39
IF (MNTH EQ 0) THEN M12=1.	40
/ END	41
/ FINISH	42
;	43

a. Line numbers do not appear in the program.

Table 6.4

Dropping out of College

Covariates	Model 1	Model 2	Model 3	Model 4	Model 5
Time-Independent Covariates					
(1) SEX	0.324	0.340†	0.380†	0.372†	0.342†
(2) GRD	0.285**	0.289***	0.274**	0.269**	0.272**
(3) PRT	1.462***	1.368***	1.063**	0.969***	1.004***
(4) LAG	0.127***	0.125***	0.084***	0.078***	0.080***
(5) PRT*LAG	-0.086*	-0.081†	-0.018	—	—
Time-Dependent Covariates					
(6) MS	—	1.255**	1.274**	1.275**	1.308**
(7) EMP	—	0.512*	0.470*	0.474*	-
(8) M1	—	—	-1.691*	-1.694*	-1.738*
M2	—	—	-1.435†	-1.427†	-1.525*
M3	—	—	-1.820*	-1.824*	-1.876*
M4	—	—	-0.714	-0.717	-0.736
M5	—	—	0.193	0.214	0.223
M7	—	—	-1.570†	-1.580†	-1.582†
M8	—	—	-0.341	-0.355	-0.392
M9	—	—	-2.240*	-2.269*	-2.348*
M10	—	—	-3.078*	-3.176*	-3.238**
M11	—	—	-2.490**	-2.568***	-2.666***
M12	—	—	-0.422	-0.436	-0.484
Global χ^2 (score)	84.67***	100.63***	136.05***	136.03***	129.82***
Wald	66.51***	80.55***	108.83***	107.58***	101.45***
L^2 (LR)	49.57***	62.70***	98.15***	97.99***	92.37***
df	5	7	18	17	16

Wald and Likelihood-Ratio Tests for Comparison of Models

		Model 1	Model 2	Model 3
Eliminate: PART*LAG	Wald	4.29*	3.44†	0.16
	L^2	5.20*	4.30*	0.16
	df	1	1	1
Eliminate: MS	Wald		8.64**	
	L^2		6.20*	
	df		1	
Eliminate: EMP	Wald		6.59*	
	L^2		6.59*	
	df		1	
Eliminate: M1-M5, M7-M12	Wald			31.20***
	L^2			35.46***
	df			11

†$p < .10$; *$p < .05$; **$p < .01$; ***$p < .001$

year. Two dummy variables rather than three were used because of the small number of events in the fourth year (see Table 6.1). The results were all insignificant except for one case in which an adequate convergence was not attained.

Interestingly, the introduction of the set of 11 month variables into Model 2 makes the interaction effect of PRT and LAG insignificant. Hence Model 4 is obtained by omitting PRT*LAG from Model 3. Model 5, which omits EMP from Model 4, is given for reference. The results of this model can be reproduced with the raw data given below.

One conspicuous characteristic of the results presented in Table 6.4 is that there are rather large discrepancies among the three chi-square tests of each model. For each model, the global chi-square, which is the score statistic, is the largest, and the likelihood-ratio chi-square is the smallest. Recall that the BMDP2L program automatically generates the score statistic, but the other two require the use of the TEST procedure (see Chapter 5). The discrepancies among the test statistics clearly indicate that the comparison of nested models should be based on more than one test. We use both the Wald test and the likelihood-ratio test to measure the significance of factors added to the model. The results of the two tests, given in Table 6.4, are fairly similar.[9] Consequently, among models that are tested here, Model 4 provides the "best" fit with the data.

Interpretation of Parameters Estimated from Model 4

Model 4 includes four time-independent covariates and two time-dependent covariates whose effects are characterized by a single parameter. Hence it may be worthwhile to examine which factors are more important than others by examining the reduction in chi-square when each factor is eliminated from the model. Although the same procedure is applied for the set of month dummy variables, this test leads to a chi-square statistic with 11 degrees of freedom, and therefore the results cannot be compared directly with other tests that have 1 degree of freedom. The Wald and likelihood-ratio chi-square test statistics presented in Table 6.5 are obtained by (a) eliminating each factor, one at a time, from Model 4 and obtaining the test statistic for this elimination; and (b) replacing the factor and repeating step (a).

Table 6.5 shows some minor inconsistencies between the two tests. Overall, however, the tests are in agreement and indicate that among covariates that use one parameter, PRT and LAG contribute to the

Table 6.5

Chi-Square Values by Omission of a Covariate from Model 4

Eliminated Covariates	Wald Test	Likelihood-Ratio Test	df
SEX	3.23†	3.32†	1
LAG	13.75***	9.60**	1
GRD	9.77**	9.42**	1
PRT	12.19***	10.24**	1
MS	8.86**	6.35*	1
EMP	5.61*	5.62*	1
M1-M5,M7-M12	34.51***	39.59***	11

†$p < .10$; *$p < .05$; **$p < .01$; ***$p < .001$.

explanatory power of the model (measured in chi-square) most strongly. GRD is the third most important factor, MS comes in fourth, EMP comes in fifth, and SEX has the least explanatory power, which is marginally significant. The distinction of months contributes to the chi-square more than any of these covariates, but uses 11 parameters. Its P level (not presented) suggests that the effect of months is about as strong as that of PRT or LAG.

Chi-square values for dichotomous covariates, however, depend on the relative size of the two categories. If the size of one category is very small, relative to the other, it will explain a small amount of chi-square even if the parameter estimate is large. Therefore, among the dichotomous covariates—SEX, PRT, MS, and EMP—a different kind of comparison is made based on the size of parameter estimates. We can see from the coefficients in Table 6.4 that the difference in the log-hazard rates between two states is strongest for MS, followed by successively smaller values for PRT, EMP, and SEX—though significant tests of differences are necessary to make a definite statement about this order.

In terms of the ratios of rates, married persons are 3.58 [= exp(1.275)] times more likely to drop out of college compared with single persons, entering college as a part-time student makes dropping out 2.64 [= exp(0.969)] times more likely than entering as a full-time student, and working 20 hours or more makes dropping out 1.61 [= exp(.474)] times more likely to occur. These results support the hypothesis discussed earlier, that role conflicts that interfere with schooling increase the risk of dropping out.

The hypothesis for educational continuity is also supported by the results. The effect of LAG indicates that each *year* of delay in entering college makes the rate of dropping out 2.55 [exp(12 × 0.078)] times greater. The hypothesis regarding academic performance is also supported by the results. For example, students who report that they received mostly Bs in high school are 1.71 [= exp(2 × 0.269)] times more likely to drop out of college than students who received mostly As in high school (see Table 6.1 for the values of GRD).

Finally, the coefficients for months indicate that dropping out of college is most likely to occur in May and June and least likely to occur during September, October, and November. Therefore, the most typical pattern of dropping out occurs when students do not return to school after the summer, and the least typical pattern is for dropping out to occur during the fall quarter/semester and before December. The hazard rate in the month of highest risk (May) is 29.67 [exp(0.214 − (−3.176)] times greater than that in the month of lowest risk (October).

CONCLUDING REMARKS

For a discussion of time-dependent covariates, see Tuma and Hannan (1984, chaps. 7, 8), Kalbfleisch and Prentice (1980, sec. 5.3), and Cox and Oakes (1984, chap. 8). For formal descriptions of techniques for handling unobserved heterogeneity, see Tuma and Hannan (1984, secs. 6.3, 6.4), Heckman and Singer (1982, 1984), and Trussell and Richards (1985). For a comparison of methods and models for unobserved heterogeneity, see Yamaguchi (1986).

PROBLEMS

(1) Using the data in Table 6.6, perform the following analysis for dropping out of college.

  (a) Replicate Model 5 of Table 6.4.

  (b) While retaining all covariates of Model 5, examine the interaction effects among time-independent covariates using stepwise regression.

  (c) Select a single time-independent covariate to use in the following tests. Assess the significance of the following interaction effects using the Wald test and the likelihood-ratio test.

Table 6.6
Raw Data Set

OBS	DUR	EVT	SEX	GRD	PRT	LAG	MRG	STM
1	41	0	1	2	0	3	99	9
2	8	1	0	4	1	3	99	9
3	41	0	1	3	0	3	99	9
4	4	1	1	4	1	2	99	8
5	47	0	0	1	0	0	99	6
6	44	0	1	2	0	3	99	9
7	39	0	1	1	0	3	99	9
8	4	1	0	5	0	2	33	8
9	21	1	0	1	0	3	99	9
10	41	0	1	4	0	3	99	9
11	3	1	1	4	0	3	47	9
12	3	1	1	1	1	3	99	9
13	20	1	0	4	1	3	99	9
14	41	0	1	2	0	3	99	9
15	3	1	1	3	0	3	99	9
16	18	1	0	1	0	6	99	12
17	40	0	0	2	0	5	99	10
18	12	1	0	2	1	5	99	10
19	40	0	0	2	0	5	99	10
20	41	0	0	2	0	3	99	9
21	30	1	0	3	0	4	99	10
22	4	1	0	4	0	3	99	8
23	11	1	0	3	0	4	99	9
51	15	1	1	3	0	3	99	9
52	27	1	0	2	0	3	99	9
53	41	0	1	3	0	3	43	9
54	8	1	1	4	0	4	30	9
55	41	0	0	2	0	4	99	9
56	23	1	1	2	0	1	99	7
57	3	1	1	4	0	3	99	9
58	41	0	1	1	0	3	99	9
59	40	0	1	3	0	4	45	10
60	40	0	1	4	0	4	48	10
61	5	1	1	2	0	4	28	10
62	26	1	1	2	0	3	99	9
63	21	1	1	2	0	3	99	9
64	30	1	1	4	0	4	99	10
65	8	1	1	1	0	3	99	9
66	41	0	1	4	0	3	99	9
67	40	0	1	2	0	4	99	10
68	1	1	1	2	0	0	2	6
69	45	0	1	2	0	4	99	9
70	40	0	1	4	0	4	99	10
71	2	1	1	3	0	4	99	10
72	41	0	1	2	0	3	99	9
73	41	0	1	3	0	3	99	9

#								
24	3	1	0	1	0	3	99	9
25	41	0	0	1	0	3	99	9
26	44	0	1	1	0	0	99	6
27	40	0	0	2	0	4	99	10
28	41	0	0	3	0	3	99	9
29	41	0	1	2	0	3	99	9
30	41	0	1	3	0	3	99	9
31	45	0	0	1	0	3	99	9
32	41	0	0	4	0	4	99	9
33	41	0	0	3	0	3	99	9
34	41	0	1	2	0	3	99	9
35	8	1	0	1	0	4	8	10
36	41	0	1	1	0	3	99	9
37	44	0	1	2	0	0	99	6
38	41	0	0	2	1	3	99	9
39	41	0	0	1	0	3	99	9
40	21	1	1	2	0	3	35	9
41	40	0	0	1	0	4	99	10
42	39	1	1	2	0	4	99	9
43	9	1	1	3	0	4	44	9
44	2	1	1	2	1	40	99	45
45	41	0	1	4	0	3	99	9
46	41	0	0	4	0	3	99	9
47	21	1	1	1	0	3	99	9
48	3	1	1	3	0	3	99	9
49	8	1	1	4	0	3	99	9
50	15	1	1	4	0	3	99	9

#								
74	41	0	0	3	0	3	99	9
75	41	0	1	1	0	3	99	9
76	41	0	0	1	0	3	29	9
77	21	1	1	1	0	3	99	9
78	41	0	0	2	0	3	99	9
79	40	1	0	5	0	3	99	9
80	41	0	1	1	0	3	99	9
81	41	0	1	2	1	3	99	9
82	41	0	0	1	0	3	99	9
83	41	0	1	3	0	3	99	9
84	41	0	1	3	0	3	99	9
85	6	1	1	4	0	0	8	6
86	44	0	0	1	0	2	99	8
87	9	1	1	1	0	8	99	13
88	0	0	0	3	0	7	99	13
89	2	1	0	2	1	3	99	9
90	32	1	1	2	1	3	99	9
91	5	1	0	2	0	1	99	6
92	44	1	1	1	0	3	99	9
93	32	0	1	4	0	4	99	9
94	41	1	0	3	0	4	99	9
95	41	0	0	1	0	4	99	10
96	40	0	0	1	0	3	99	9
97	41	0	0	2	0	4	99	9
98	41	0	1	2	0	5	99	10
99	7	1	1	1	0	5	18	9
100	21	1	0	2	0	3	99	9

Continued

Table 6.6, Continued

OBS	DUR	EVT	SEX	GRD	PRT	LAG	MRG	STM	OBS	DUR	EVT	SEX	GRD	PRT	LAG	MRG	STM
101	39	1	0	3	0	3	99	9	151	41	0	0	4	0	3	42	9
102	41	0	0	1	0	0	99	9	152	2	1	0	1	1	0	99	6
103	42	0	0	1	1	2	99	8	153	2	1	1	3	1	0	99	6
104	41	0	0	4	0	3	99	9	154	9	1	1	1	0	3	37	9
105	42	0	0	1	0	2	99	8	155	45	0	1	2	0	3	99	9
106	7	1	1	2	1	3	6	9	156	10	1	1	3	0	3	99	9
107	42	0	1	1	0	2	99	8	157	44	0	1	2	0	0	99	6
108	5	1	1	5	1	15	99	21	158	41	0	1	1	0	3	99	9
109	41	0	0	1	0	3	99	9	159	41	0	1	1	0	3	99	9
110	41	0	0	1	0	3	99	9	160	41	0	1	2	0	3	99	9
111	41	0	0	2	0	3	99	9	161	33	1	1	1	0	3	43	9
112	9	1	1	3	0	3	99	9	162	21	1	1	1	0	3	99	9
113	41	0	0	3	0	3	99	9	163	41	0	1	2	0	3	99	9
114	44	0	1	2	0	0	99	6	164	42	0	0	3	0	2	99	8
115	2	1	0	5	1	0	99	6	165	41	0	0	1	0	3	99	9
116	15	1	0	3	0	0	99	6	166	34	1	1	1	0	3	20	9
117	41	0	1	2	0	4	99	9	167	27	1	1	2	0	3	99	9
118	41	0	1	3	0	4	99	9	168	41	0	0	1	0	3	99	9
119	41	0	0	3	0	3	99	9	169	41	0	1	1	0	3	99	9
120	2	1	0	2	0	33	99	39	170	8	1	1	4	0	3	38	9
121	41	0	0	2	0	3	99	9	171	6	1	1	3	0	2	33	8
122	9	1	1	2	1	3	99	9	172	41	0	1	1	0	3	99	9
123	33	1	1	1	0	3	47	9	173	33	1	0	1	0	3	99	9
124	9	1	1	1	0	3	24	9	174	44	0	1	1	0	3	99	6

125	41	0	1	1	0	3	99	9
126	41	0	1	1	0	3	44	9
127	40	0	0	3	0	4	99	10
128	41	0	1	2	0	3	99	9
129	41	0	1	1	0	3	99	9
130	29	1	0	2	0	3	99	9
131	41	0	1	3	0	3	99	9
132	41	0	1	3	0	3	99	9
133	41	0	1	1	0	3	99	9
134	44	0	0	1	1	0	99	6
135	9	1	1	3	0	2	99	8
136	41	0	0	1	0	3	99	9
137	44	1	1	1	0	4	99	10
138	44	0	0	1	0	0	99	6
139	8	1	1	3	0	3	99	9
140	44	0	1	1	0	3	99	9
141	41	0	0	2	0	3	99	9
142	41	0	0	2	0	2	99	8
143	42	0	1	2	0	3	99	9
144	41	0	0	1	0	3	18	9
145	41	0	1	1	0	4	99	9
146	32	0	0	1	0	3	99	10
147	4	1	1	1	0	2	99	21
148	42	0	1	3	0	2	99	8
149	10	1	0	3	0	1	99	7
150	41	0	1	1	0	3	99	9

175	21	1	0	1	0	3	99	9
176	41	0	1	1	0	3	99	9
177	41	0	1	2	0	3	99	9
178	41	0	0	1	0	3	99	9
179	42	0	0	3	0	2	99	8
180	43	0	0	1	0	1	99	7
181	44	0	0	1	0	0	99	6
182	41	0	1	2	0	3	99	9
183	41	0	0	2	0	3	99	9
184	2	1	1	5	1	0	30	6
185	1	1	0	3	0	43	99	49
186	41	0	0	2	0	3	99	9
187	41	0	1	2	0	3	99	9
188	41	0	1	1	0	3	99	9
189	40	0	0	1	0	4	99	10
190	8	1	0	3	0	15	99	21
191	11	1	1	1	0	3	99	9
192	41	0	0	2	0	3	99	9
193	41	0	1	2	0	3	99	9
194	33	1	0	3	0	3	40	9
195	41	0	1	3	0	3	99	9
196	42	0	0	1	0	2	99	8
197	41	0	0	1	0	3	99	9
198	20	1	1	3	0	3	99	9
199	41	0	0	1	0	3	99	9
200	41	1	1	2	0	3	99	9

Continued

Table 6.6, Continued

OBS	DUR	EVT	SEX	GRD	PRT	LAG	MRG	STM
201	42	0	0	2	1	2	99	8
202	41	0	0	2	0	3	99	9
203	29	0	1	1	0	15	99	21
204	41	0	1	2	0	3	99	9
205	41	0	0	2	0	3	99	9
206	27	1	1	3	0	3	99	9
207	17	1	1	2	0	2	99	8
208	41	0	1	3	0	3	99	9
209	14	1	1	4	0	4	99	10
210	33	1	0	4	0	3	99	9
211	36	1	1	2	1	3	99	9
212	41	0	1	2	0	3	99	9
213	31	1	1	1	0	3	99	9
214	9	1	0	1	0	2	99	8
215	44	0	1	2	0	0	99	6
216	24	1	0	1	0	2	99	8
217	2	1	1	3	0	3	99	9
218	6	1	0	2	0	3	99	9
219	9	1	0	3	0	2	99	8
220	41	0	1	2	0	3	99	9
221	41	0	1	2	0	30	99	9
222	41	0	1	3	0	30	99	9
223	4	1	0	4	1	80	99	14
224	21	1	1	2	0	30	99	9

OBS	DUR	EVT	SEX	GRD	PRT	LAG	MRG	STM
236	41	0	1	2	0	30	99	9
237	9	1	1	2	0	30	99	9
238	21	1	0	3	0	30	99	9
239	32	1	1	2	0	30	12	9
240	41	0	1	1	0	30	99	9
241	41	0	1	2	0	30	99	9
242	41	0	1	4	0	30	99	9
243	41	0	0	3	0	30	99	9
244	40	0	0	1	0	40	99	10
245	41	0	1	1	0	30	99	9
246	41	0	1	4	0	30	99	9
247	41	0	1	3	0	30	99	9
248	41	0	1	3	0	30	99	9
249	41	0	0	4	0	30	99	9
250	41	0	1	4	0	30	99	9
251	41	0	0	3	0	30	99	9
252	20	1	0	5	0	30	99	9
253	7	1	1	1	0	30	99	9
254	41	0	1	2	0	30	99	9
255	41	0	1	1	0	30	99	9
256	41	0	1	2	1	30	99	9
257	41	0	1	1	0	30	99	9
258	4	1	0	2	0	30	99	9
259	3	1	1	2	0	30	99	9

225	44	0	1	2	0	0	99	6
226	41	0	0	3	0	30	99	9
227	33	1	1	1	0	30	99	9
228	41	0	1	1	0	30	99	9
229	41	0	0	2	0	30	99	9
230	41	0	0	1	0	30	99	9
231	3	1	1	4	1	30	99	14
232	36	0	0	5	1	80	99	10
233	40	0	0	4	0	40	99	10
234	4	1	0	2	0	40	99	8
235	42	0	1	3	0	20	99	

260	16	1	1	5	0	30	99	9
261	41	0	1	1	0	30	99	9
262	2	1	0	2	0	30	99	9
263	41	0	0	3	0	30	99	9
264	41	1	1	1	0	30	99	9
265	20	1	1	2	0	20	99	8

(i) interaction effect of the covariate with TIME

(ii) interaction effect of the covariate with D2 and D3, where D2 and D3 contrast the second year and the combination of the third and fourth years, respectively, against the first year

(2) Based on the data in Table 6.6, use BMDP2L for the following analysis of getting married. Note that this analysis is given only as a practice exercise—it contains two methodological problems. Problems (a) and (b) below address these problems, and problems (c) through (i) are concerned with the analysis of the event.

(a) It is obvious that this analysis does not represent a subpopulation of people who do not go to college. However, is there any other problem in the selection of the sample over and beyond this issue of generalizability? To answer this question, consider the following two situations. In Society A, people do not get married before leaving high school, they do not return to school once they leave, and they do not go to college unless they do so immediately after high school graduation. Accordingly, marriage is always determined after the decision to go or not go to college. In Society B, people may get married before leaving high school, or they may enter college after marriage at a time other than immediately after high school graduation. It is adequate to analyze getting married among college entrants for Society A, but not adequate for Society B. Explain why. (Hint: Review the discussion on sample selection in the chapter subsection headed "State-Dependent Covariates.")

(b) We assume here that everybody enters the risk set for marriage in January 1980. Is the assumption adequate for this data set? If it is not, explain why it is not, and provide a better definition of the risk period if relevant variables were available. If it is nearly adequate for the present case, is such a definition always adequate for different data sets? Explain why. (Hint: The present sample includes only one cohort.)

(c) Observations are terminated for persons who never married as of February 1984. Compute the dependent variable for duration of being single after January 1980. Also compute the status variable that distinguishes the occurrence of the event from censored observations. Note that variable MRG is based on the year-month code that takes a value of 0 for January 1980 and that the variable is coded 99 if the subject is never married.

(d) Apply the proportional hazards model using SEX and GRD as covariates.

(e) In this analysis, we cannot use PRT and LAG as time-independent covariates. Explain why.

(f) Create a time-dependent covariate that represents ever having dropped out of college and enter this covariate into the model. Note that STM+DUR becomes the year-month of dropping out if EVT = 1.

(g) Examine the interaction effects among covariates.

(h) Examine nonproportional effects by testing the interaction effects of each covariate and TIME.

(i) Interpret the results from the best-fitting model among the models tested above.

NOTES

1. Compared with linear regression analysis, unobserved heterogeneity is a more serious problem in event history analyses that employ proportional hazards models and/or their extensions. In linear regression analyses, omitted variables that affect the dependent variable do not cause any bias in parameter estimates if they are uncorrelated with the included explanatory variables. By contrast, omitted variables that influence hazard rates in proportional hazards models do cause bias in parameter estimates even if they are initially uncorrelated with the included covariates (Trussell & Richards, 1985).

2. The renewal process model here is different from the modulated renewal process model discussed in Chapter 3 because the former model cannot employ covariates that characterize interdependence among spells, such as covariates that reflect outcomes of the preceding spells.

3. The use of right-censored spells generates bias because it is always the last spell for each subject. In other words, right censoring is not independent of the order of spells, and therefore covariates may obtain biased effects simply due to their association with the order of spells.

4. A general method for detecting misspecification of the hazard-rate model has recently been advocated by Arminger (1988).

5. Hence we should not set sample selection criteria according to the outcome of the dependent process. For example, we should not analyze marriage as an event only among people who ever married. This explains why excluding right-censored cases generates bias.

6. Rate-dependent covariates include cases, as in this medical example, where the availability of the covariate value itself at time t indicates survival up to time t. Therefore, the conditional survival probability at time t for a given value of this covariate becomes one (Kalbfleisch & Prentice, 1980). Hence the covariate cannot be handled by the regular formulation of the likelihood function. There are some estimation problems for models with such covariates.

7. In order to solve the problem, Lillard and Waite (1990) modeled the hazard rates of two events, marital disruption and birth spacing, simultaneously. In their model, the hazard rate of birth spacing depends directly on the hazard rate of marital disruption, while the hazard rate of marital disruption depends on the state of preceding births (which is a rate-dependent covariate).

8. Other covariates that were considered in earlier analysis but excluded from the current application because of their insignificance include father's education, family income, public versus private college, and a distinction between working and not working.

9. Wald tests were also conducted for the possible significance of factors that were deleted by the stepwise regression procedure because the stepwise procedure is based only on the likelihood-ratio test. The results do not differ between the two tests.

7

Final Remarks Before Getting One's Own Research Started

In this chapter, the modeling of substantive phenomena is linked to the prevalent methodological considerations in event history analysis. The discussion includes both a brief review of selected topics that appeared in preceding chapters as well as a discussion of some new topics. However, the issues of unobserved heterogeneity and selection bias presented in Chapter 6 are not repeated here.

RISK PERIOD

It is obvious that we need to know when subjects are at risk for having the event in order to analyze the hazard rate for the event. Indeed, for almost all event history analyses, we assume knowledge of the exact timing of entry into the risk period. In certain cases, however, the real risk period may not be ascertained clearly. Three different situations are identified below, and solutions for each situation are discussed.

Events That Have Logically Preceding Events

There are two major ways to define the beginning of the risk period in social science research. One major type is used for events whose risk period starts when subjects enter a particular life state. For example, the risk period for divorce begins when subjects marry. Similarly, the risk period for dropping out of college begins with matriculation. These events have little ambiguity regarding the beginning of the risk period. For other types of events, however, we usually do not know exactly when the risk period begins. Conventionally, we often assume that the risk period starts at a certain same age/month/date for all subjects. Events that are usually analyzed with this assumption include the first occurrence of marriage, premarital cohabitation, arrest, and the use of illicit drugs.

For some events in the second group, however, it may be rather crude to assume that all subjects enter the risk period at the same age/month/day. Premarital pregnancy is an example of such an event, because the real risk period never starts prior to the occurrence of puberty or the first premarital sexual intercourse. At the same time, the timing of puberty or the first premarital sexual intercourse may vary considerably among subjects. Hence, if we have data on the timing of the first premarital sexual intercourse, for example, it is best to divide the analysis into two steps. In the first step, we model the hazard rate of having the first premarital sexual intercourse by assuming that all subjects enter the risk period at the same age/month/day. In the second step, we model the hazard rate of becoming premaritally pregnant by assuming that the risk period begins with the subject-specific date of the first premarital sexual intercourse.

Hogan and Kitagawa (1985), in fact, have used such a two-step analysis of premarital pregnancy. This two-step technique is advantageous because it elaborates the specification for each risk period and therefore provides richer information about the occurrence of each dependent event. Certain covariates, such as juvenile delinquency, may affect the first event (premarital sexual intercourse) but not the second (premarital pregnancy). Certain other covariates, such as knowledge about contraceptives, may affect only the second event.

Generally, the use of the two-step analysis is recommended if (a) there is a logically preceding event before which the risk of the event of interest is zero, and (b) the timing of the logically preceding event is known for each subject.

Events for Which Only the Average Length of the Real Risk Period per Unit of Observed Time Is Available

I describe this situation with a concrete example. Think of analyzing the occurrence of automobile accidents among drivers. Strictly speaking, people are at risk for having the event only when they are driving. However, the researcher may not have data on the beginning and end of each risk period, but may have data on the average hours of driving per week. The data approximate the average amount of real risk per unit of observed time. Hence one may assume that, other things being equal, twice as many driving hours generate twice as much hazard rate, or, more generally, hazard rates depend proportionally on the hours of driving per week. Then one can exclude from the analysis subjects who never drive and introduce the average hours of driving per week as a covariate in the proportional hazards model for the remaining subjects.

A caveat is necessary, however, when factors that affect the hazard rate include not only the hours of driving per week but also the cumulative hours of driving—that is, driving experience. If we used the real risk period, driving time, to define the baseline hazard rate, the effect of driving experience would simply represent duration dependence. However, when the average hours of driving per unit of time is used as a covariate, the correct model has to account separately for the effect of cumulative hours of driving or its proxy measure for driving experience.

Events with Truncated Duration Dependence

Generally, event history analysis is most suitable for events in which the timing of entry into the risk period and the timing of the event are accurately measured. In this regard, the analysis of attitudinal change or change in psychological states is usually inappropriate for event history analysis because we have neither of these timing data. The second problem, the timing of the event, can be solved by defining the event as a change in the state at a predetermined point in time, as in panel data analysis. However, it is always difficult to identify the beginning of the current state for such variables, and therefore we have the problem of left censoring. As discussed in Chapter 3, however, we can often assume that duration dependence is truncated in such a way that, over and beyond a fixed amount of duration, any further duration does not change the amount of duration dependence. Then we can use attitudinal/psychological states as a dependent variable in a model that adequately accounts for the time-lagged effects of the dependent variable, and analyze the determinants of the odds of transition between states.

TEMPORAL ORDER

Temporal order is a necessary condition for making a causal inference in event history analysis. By taking a time lag for the measurement of time-dependent covariates, temporal order can be established between the realization of covariate states and the occurrence of the event. However, this temporal order is not sufficient for causal direction to be established. In the case of rate-dependent covariates, discussed in Chapter 6, the covariate process is influenced directly by hazard rates of the dependent process, and therefore reverse causation exists. However, for certain situations, including anticipatory socialization (also discussed in Chapter 6), the rate dependence of a time-dependent covariate may exist only for a certain time interval prior to the occurrence of the event. Then we can use a longer time lag for the covariate to solve the problem (for an example, see Yamaguchi & Kandel, 1985b).

TIMING OF ENTRY INTO THE RISK PERIOD AND TIMING OF TRANSITIONS IN COVARIATE STATES

Another salient aspect in the analysis of event history data is the timing of events as predictors of other events. In particular, the timing of entry into a life state (where the entry represents an event) may affect the hazard rate of leaving the state (which represents another event). An example is the effect of age at marriage on the occurrence of divorce. A very early age of marriage is known to be associated with a high hazard rate of divorce (Bumpass & Sweet, 1972; Fergusson et al., 1984; Morgan & Rindfuss, 1985; Teachman, 1982).

A slightly different example, which was presented in Chapter 6, is the effect of the time lag between entry into college and graduation from high school on the hazard rate for dropping out of college. The longer time lag predicted a higher hazard rate of dropping out. In this case, it is not the absolute timing but the relative timing, or *spacing*, of two events (i.e., high school graduation and entry into college) that affects the occurrence of the third event (dropping out of college). The second event represents the entry into the risk period of the third event here.

Generally, if there is a "normative" spacing between the first two events, a deviation from it may affect the occurrence of a third event, which usually represents a negative outcome. Another example of this type is the effect of the length of unemployment prior to the first employment on the hazard rate of unemployment in the future. The initial unemployment characterizes a time lag between entry into the labor force (the first event) and the first employment (the second event). A longer time lag predicts a higher hazard rate for another unemployment (the third event) (Heckman & Borjas, 1980).

A different aspect of timing may also influence the hazard rate, namely, the timing of transitions in covariate states. For example, in Chapter 2 we saw that among subjects who started their first employment at relatively late ages, being employed had a larger effect on the hazard rate of marriage, compared with subjects who started their first employment at relatively early ages. Hence the timing of employment affects the hazard rate of marriage. The spacing of transitions in covariate states also affects the hazard rate. For example, marriages in which there is relatively short spacing between pregnancies or births have a higher rate of divorce (LaRossa & LaRossa, 1981; Rossi, 1968).

In summary, both the absolute timing, or the relative timing (i.e., spacing), of entry into the risk period for the dependent event and the timing and spacing of transitions in covariate states may affect the hazard rate. It is worthwhile to explore such timing and spacing effects in formulating substantive hypotheses.

DURATION DEPENDENCE AND COVARIATE DURATION EFFECTS

As in the case of the timing of events, we can distinguish two distinct aspects of duration dependence. One pertains to the effect of the duration of the state at risk for the dependent process, which has been referred to here as duration dependence. The other pertains to the duration for a covariate state. We refer to its effects on the hazard rate as *covariate duration effects.*

An example of the first case was introduced in Chapter 4. As employees stay in a firm longer, they are less likely, on the average, to leave the firm. This duration effect on employment stability, which exists probably because firm-specific human capital increases with duration of employment, has been documented in many studies (e.g., DiPrete, 1981; Kandel & Yamaguchi, 1987; Sørensen & Tuma, 1981; Tuma, 1976). Another example of duration dependence can be found in the "age" effects on organizational death rates (Carroll, 1985; Freeman, Carroll, & Hannan, 1983). Firms become less likely to "die" as their ages increase. A negative duration effect of marriage on the hazard rate of divorce also exists (e.g., Morgan & Rindfuss, 1985). As discussed in Chapter 6, however, negative duration dependence may be overestimated because of the possible confounding effect of unobserved population heterogeneity.

An example of a covariate duration effect is the effect of the "duration of parenthood," including the period of pregnancy that precedes a birth, on the hazard rate of voluntary job leaves among married women. The duration of parenthood represents the time-continuous age of the first child.

A simple parametric characterization for duration dependence is unlikely to attain a good fit with social science data, as has been shown in several examples in this volume. Similar situations will exist for a covariate duration effect. Therefore, it is worth employing first a step-functional characterization for the effect without rigidly specifying its functional form.

IDENTIFICATION PROBLEMS

The importance of the effects of both the timing and duration of states for the dependent variable and covariates cannot be overemphasized. However, an identification problem arises if the researcher includes both the effects of timing and duration simultaneously with the effect of time.

For example, we cannot easily estimate the simultaneous effects on the hazard rate of (a) age, as a time-dependent covariate; (b) the age of entry into the risk period; and (c) the duration of the risk period. Similarly, we cannot easily estimate the simultaneous effects of (a) age, (b) the age at which a covariate enters a particular state, and (c) the duration of this covariate state. The problem in both examples is identical to the well-known problem in the simultaneous estimation of age, cohort, and period effects. Since knowledge of any two determines the third, the three effects are not estimable simultaneously unless the researcher makes some assumptions to avoid their complete functional interdependence. Techniques that are employed to deal with this issue are beyond the scope of this book (for analysis of age, period, and cohort effects, see Glenn, 1977; Mason & Fienberg, 1985). The easiest solution, although it will not be the best one, is to omit one of the three effects in considering their theoretical relevance.

INTERACTION EFFECTS INVOLVING
DURATION DEPENDENCE AND
THE DURATION OF COVARIATE STATES

Not only are the duration of the risk period and that of covariate states important, but their possible interactions with other covariates in determining hazard rates may have important theoretical implications. The presence of interaction effects between a covariate and the duration of the risk period requires the use of nonproportional hazards models. A few examples have been presented that use this type of interaction effect. In Chapter 4 the interaction effect of employment duration and firm size on the hazard rates of interfirm mobility was hypothesized and confirmed. Similarly, in Chapter 2 the interaction effect of age (or the duration of being never married) and employment in predicting the hazard rates of getting married was hypothesized and confirmed. Morgan and Rindfuss (1985) found significant interaction effects of marriage duration and the sequencing of conception, birth, and marriage on the hazard rates of divorce.

The interaction effect of the duration of a covariate state and another covariate may also be found in many studies. Suppose that co-residence with parents of the wife or husband reduces voluntary job leaves among married women because parents can take care of babies. This will lead to an interaction effect of co-residence and the duration of parenthood on the hazard rate of voluntary job leaves among married women.

Generally, the interaction effects between covariates and time (or duration) for either the dependent process or the covariate process have important theoretical implications. Researchers will find it beneficial to explore, construct, and test hypotheses that pertain to these interaction effects.

MULTIDIMENSIONAL TIME EFFECTS

Hazard rates of events that are analyzed in social science research often depend on more than one dimension of time. Examples of events with multiple dimensions of time effects are given in the illustrative analyses in Chapters 3 and 6, that is, the period and duration effects for the analysis of changes in personal efficacy, and the duration and cyclic month effects in the analysis of dropping out of college. Tuma and Hannan (1984, chap. 7) discuss the use of distinct time dimensions, including age, historical period, duration of the risk period, and experience (such as cumulative labor force participation in the analysis of job separations as a repeatable event).

Two remarks are worth making here. First, time effects, whether period, age, duration, or experience, may not take a simple linear or curvilinear form. On the other hand, this does not imply that all time effects take the form of some complicated function and always require either a nonparametric control or a step-functional approximation. For example, the cyclic month effects that are used in the analysis in Chapter 6 are a special form of the period effect, but a rather simple one. Similarly, the effects of time-lagged states of the dependent variable that are used in Chapter 3, with the assumption of truncated duration dependence, are a specific nonlinear effect of duration. The form is again simple.

Second, if we can assume *linear* effects on log-hazard rates for more than one dimension of continuous time in the model, we may be able to simplify the analysis by replacing some time-continuous covariates with either time-independent covariates or covariates that do not change with time within spells. For example, in the analysis of a remarriage after the first divorce, we may assume both the linear effects of individual age and duration of divorce on log-hazard rates such that

$$h_i(t) = \exp\left[a + \sum_j b_j x_j + c_1 D_i(t) + c_2 A_i(t)\right] \qquad (7.1)$$

where $A_i(t)$ and $D_i(t)$ are individual age and duration of divorce, respectively. Then this model becomes equivalent to the following model:

$$h_i(t) = \exp\left[a + \sum_j b_j x_j + d_1 D_i(t) + d_2 A_i\right] \qquad (7.2)$$

where A_i is age at divorce and does not depend on time. Here, $d_1 = c_1 + c_2$ and $d_2 = c_2$ hold true between the parameter estimates of the two models. It follows that we can obtain parameter estimates of c_1 and c_2 and their standard errors from the estimates of d_1 and d_2 and their variance-covariance matrix.

Similarly, Tuma and Hannan (1984, pp. 217-218) discuss in the analysis of job separation as a repeatable event the use of covariates that change their values only across spells—namely, age and experience (i.e., cumulative job duration) measured at the beginning of each employment spell—instead of time-dependent covariates for age and experience. Again, parameter estimates require a translation for the effects of job duration and time-varying effects of age and experience.[1]

The advantages of Formula 7.2 compared with 7.1 are that (a) the models can be applied with a computer program that permits only one time-continuous explanatory variable and (b) the models are much less costly in terms of computational requirements.

At the same time, we should not take advantage of this reparameterization trick mechanically. The assumption that each time variable has a linear effect on log-hazard rates is very strong. Researchers should first test the adequacy of the linear effect for each time variable included in the model.

COMPETING EVENTS

Competing events are different events that can occur within the same risk period. Typical examples include the occurrence of voluntary versus involuntary job leaves, job losses versus job changes, and separation from the cohabitation partner versus marriage to the partner. In each case, the occurrence of an event implies the termination of the risk period for the other event. In other cases, the risk period for event A may continue in spite of the occurrence of event B, while the risk period for event B is terminated by the occurrence of event A. Examples include interfirm versus intrafirm job separations, across-state versus within-state migration, and marriage versus premarital cohabitation. Here subjects who experience the second event are still at risk for having the first event, but once subjects experience the first event, they are no longer at risk for having the second event.

Technically speaking, there are two ideal situations where the competing events can be analyzed with little methodological difficulty. In one ideal situation, which I refer to as a *type I* situation, each one of the multiple competing events occurs in two steps. The first step characterizes the occurrence of any one of the multiple events, and the second step characterizes the occurrence of a particular event, given that some event has occurred. It is assumed here that multiple events share the same process as the first step, and that competition among the events occurs only for the second step. Formally, this situation requires that the two steps do not have any common parameters, although they can involve common covariates. In many cases, the two steps reflect a conceptual rather than an empirical distinction, since the occurrence of an event simultaneously determines which particular event occurs. An example of this type is job promotion classified by type of promotion. The first step is the occurrence of a promotion and the second step determines its type, given that a promotion has occurred. Another example is marriage classified by type of marriage, such as inter- and intraethnic marriages. The first step is the occurrence of marriage and the second step determines its type, given the occurrence of marriage.

In some cases, a logically preceding event exists for all competing events, and the competing events, in fact, represent distinct outcomes of the preceding event. An example of this type involves the three possible outcomes that follow premarital pregnancy: premarital childbirth, postmarital childbirth (i.e., marriage prior to childbirth), and abortion. The first step is the occurrence of premarital pregnancy, and the second step is the determination of its outcome, given an occurrence of premarital pregnancy.

For all these situations, one can apply a two-step analysis. For the first step, the hazard-rate model is employed for the occurrence of the generalized event, that is, the event that includes all competing events. For the second step, one may use a logit or multinomial logit model to analyze the occurrence of a particular competing event, given the occurrence of a generalized event. Yamaguchi and Kandel (1987) employed a two-step analysis for the occurrence of premarital pregnancy and its outcomes using this procedure.

An important extension of the two-step analysis has recently been introduced by Petersen (1988), who considers a dependent process with a continuous-state space. When the event occurs, its new state is determined as a value in the continuous-state space. An example is a change in socioeconomic status. While a subject holds the same occupation in the same firm or changes to the same occupation in a different firm, the duration of his or her socioeconomic status, as indicated by occupation, continues. When a subject changes his or her occupation, either within the firm or across firms, a change in socioeconomic status occurs. The new state is the socioeconomic status of the new occupation.

Under the assumption that parameters are independent between the first step, which determines the duration of the current occupation, and the second step, which determines the new socioeconomic status, given a change of occupation, one can apply a hazard-rate model for the first step and a linear regression analysis for the second step. The second step uses the socioeconomic status of the new occupation as the dependent variable and the socioeconomic status of the old occupation as one of the explanatory variables. Other explanatory variables for the second step may include variables that characterize preceding work histories, including the duration of the previous occupation, as well as individual attributes.

In the second ideal situation, which I refer to as *type II*, each of the multiple events has an independent set of parameters that determines its occurrence—although, again, each event may involve the same covariates. In many cases, we may have to make this assumption in the analysis of a particular event when competing events are present. If any events other than the event of interest occur, thereby removing subjects from the risk set of the event of interest, then the occurrences of the events are all treated as censored observations.

The assumption that the occurrences of other events can be treated as censored observations, however, is not adequate if the hazard rates for multiple events have some parameters in common. One example of such parametric interdependence is found where the hazard rate of one event directly influences the hazard rate of another event. Then, all parameters of the former event become a subset of the parameters of the latter event.

Another example of parametric interdependence occurs when multiple events reflect characteristics of both type I and type II situations. In other words, occurrences of multiple events are partly determined as a two-step process and partly determined independently of other events. Voluntary job separations by type of reasons for leaving the job may be an example of such competing events because some subjects may have multiple reasons, such as job dissatisfaction and family responsibility, that jointly cause their job separations and the particular reason given in the survey may involve a distinct process of response determination (i.e., type I situation). Among other subjects, different reasons may independently cause their job separations (type II situation). If there is parametric interdependence, we have to model a set of outcome-specific hazards rates with common parameters and estimate all parameters of the multiple events simultaneously.

INDIRECT EFFECTS

A conceptually new aspect of indirect effects of life events on other life events has become apparent from event history analysis. In the traditional conceptualization, an indirect effect of variable A on variable C exists if variable A influences variable B and variable B influences variable C. While this aspect of indirect effects also applies to event history analysis, a distinct kind of indirect effect exists when a variable influences the length of the risk period of having an event and thereby influences the lifetime probability of having the event.

For example, Yamaguchi and Kandel (1985a) found that using marijuana tends to lead to a postponement of marriage, controlling for education and other determinants of the timing of marriage. Hence marijuana use has an indirect effect on the occurrence of premarital cohabitation *by postponing the termination of the risk period* of premarital cohabitation. That is, premarital cohabitation is more likely to occur for marijuana users because they remain single for a longer period of time. Similarly, marijuana use—which increases the hazard rates of experiencing the first premarital sexual intercourse—indirectly affects the occurrence of premarital pregnancy by *accelerating the timing of entry into the risk period* of premarital pregnancy.

Generally, a variable can indirectly influence the occurrence of an event by either accelerating or postponing the timing of entry into, or exit from, the risk period of having the event. Although the variable may not affect the hazard rate for the event directly, it affects the occurrence of the event indirectly by changing the length of the risk period for the event.

A related type of indirect effect changes the timing of entry into or exit from the *period of high or low risk*. Suppose there is a time-dependent covariate that affects the hazard rate of the dependent event. Then other variables that influence entry into or exit from states of the time-dependent covariate have an indirect effect on the hazard rate. For example, higher father's occupational status leads to a longer period of children's full-time education, which is a low-risk period for getting married. Thus, by lengthening the low-risk period (i.e., the period of full-time education), father's status indirectly affects the hazard rate of getting married.

Another example of indirect effects that change the period of high or low risk is found for the initiation of illicit drug use. Certain time-varying variables such as being single and having drug-using friends increase the rate of initiating the use of illicit drugs. Post-high school education plays a role here. By lengthening the period of being single and keeping youth in a social context that is particularly susceptible to peer influence, post-high school education lengthens the high-risk period for the initiation of illicit drug use. Hence, although students who plan to go to college have a lower rate of illicit drug initiation while in high school compared with other students, they "catch up" during the subsequent few years (Backman, O'Malley, & Johnston, 1984). Accordingly, post-high school education indirectly influences the hazard rate of initiating illicit drug use.

Through event history analysis, the importance of indirect effects, which operate by influencing either the timing of entry into or exit from the risk period or the timing of entry into or exit from the period of high or low risk, has been recognized.

CONCLUDING NOTES

A discussion of competing events is given by Allison (1982). More formal and in-depth discussions of competing risks are presented by Kalbfleisch and Prentice (1980, chap. 7), Cox and Oakes (1984, chap. 9), and Heckman and Honore (1989). For further discussion on multidimensional time dependence, see Tuma and Hannan (1984, chap. 7). For the two-step analysis with a continuous-state space, see Petersen (1988). Refer to Yamaguchi (1987a) for a discussion of various topics related to those presented in this chapter.

NOTE

1. The first model with three time-varying variables becomes

$$h_i(t) = \exp\left[a + \sum_j b_j x_j + c_1 D_i(t) + c_2 A_i(t) + c_3 E_i(t) \right]$$

where $D_i(t)$, $A_i(t)$, and $E_i(t)$ are, respectively, job duration, age, and experience (cumulative job duration) for subject i. The second model becomes

$$h_i(t) = \exp\left[a + \sum_j b_j x_j + d_1 D_i(t) + d_2 A_i(n) + d_3 E_i(n)\right]$$

where $A_i(n)$ and $E_i(n)$ are age and experience measured at the beginning of the nth spell for subject i. Then the equalities $d_1 = c_1 + c_2 + c_3$, $d_2 = c_2$, and $d_3 = c_3$ hold true.

References

Agresti, A. (1990). *Categorical data analysis*. New York: John Wiley.

Akaike, H. (1974). A new look at the statistical model identification. *IEEE Transactions on Automatic Control, AC-19*(6), 716-723.

Allison, P. D. (1982). Discrete-time methods for the analysis of event-histories. In S. Leinhardt (Ed.), *Sociological methodology 1982* (pp. 61-98). San Francisco: Jossey-Bass.

Allison, P. D. (1984). *Event history analysis*. Beverly Hills, CA: Sage.

Allison, P. D. (1987). Introducing a disturbance into logit and probit regression models. *Sociological Methods & Research, 15*, 355-374.

Amemiya, T., & Nold, F. (1975). A modified logit model. *Review of Economics and Statistics, 57*, 255-257.

Andersen, P. K., & Gill, R. D. (1982). Cox's regression model for counting processes: A large sample study. *Annals of Statistics, 10*, 1100-1120.

Arminger, G. (1984). Analysis of event histories with generalized linear models. In A. Diekman & P. Mitter (Eds.), *Stochastic modeling of social processes* (pp. 245-282). Orlando, FL: Academic Press.

Arminger, G. (1988). Testing misspecification in parametric rate models. In K. U. Meyer & N. B. Tuma (Eds.), *Applications of event history analysis in life course research* (pp. 679-699). Madison: University of Wisconsin Press.

Backman, J. D., O'Malley, P. M., & Johnston, L. D. (1984). Drug use among young adults: The impacts of role status and social environment. *Journal of Personality and Social Psychology, 47*, 629-645.

Bartholomew, D. J. (1982). *Stochastic models for social processes* (3rd ed.). New York: John Wiley.

Blau, P. M., & Duncan, O. D. (1967). *The American occupational structure*. New York: John Wiley.

Blossfeld, H. P., & Hamerle, A. (1989). Using Cox models to study multiepisode processes. *Sociological Methods & Research, 17*, 432-448.

Blossfeld, H. P., Hamerle, A., & Mayer, K. U. (1989). *Event history analysis*. Hillsdale, NJ: Lawrence Erlbaum.

Brown, C. C. (1975). On the use of indicator variables for studying the time dependence of parameters in a response-time model. *Biometrics, 31*, 863-872.

Bumpass, L., & Sweet, J. (1972). Differentials in marital instability: 1970. *American Sociological Review, 37*, 754-766.

Bye, B. V., & Riley, G. F. (1989). Model estimation when observations are not independent. *Sociological Methods & Research, 17*, 353-375.

Carroll, G. R. (1985). Concentration and specification: Dynamics of niche width in populations of organizations. *American Journal of Sociology, 90*, 1262-1283.

Carroll, G. R., & Mayer, K. U. (1986). Job-shifts patterns in the Federal Republic of Germany: The effects of social class, industrial sector, and organizational size. *American Sociological Review, 51*, 323-341.

Chamberlain, G. (1980). Analysis of covariance with qualitative data. *Review of Economic Studies, 47*, 225-238.

Chamberlain, G. (1985). Heterogeneity, omitted variable bias, and duration dependence. In J. J. Heckman & B. Singer (Eds.), *Longitudinal analysis of labor market data* (pp. 3-38). Cambridge: Cambridge University Press. (Original work published 1979)

Clogg, C. C. (1986). Invoked by RATE. *American Journal of Sociology, 92*, 696-706.

Clogg, C. C., & Eliason, S. R. (1987). Some common problems in log-linear analysis. *Sociological Methods & Research, 15*, 8-44.

Cole, R. E. (1973). Functional alternatives and economic development: An empirical example of permanent employment in Japan. *American Sociological Review, 26*, 615-630.

Cole, R. E. (1979). *Work, mobility, and participation.* Berkeley: University of California Press.

Coleman, J. S. (1964). *Introduction to mathematical sociology.* Glencoe, IL: Free Press.

Coleman, J. S. (1981). *Longitudinal data analysis.* New York: Basic Books.

Coleman, J. S., & Hoffer, T. (1987). *Public and private high schools: The impact of communities.* New York: Basic Books.

Coleman, J. S., Hoffer, T., & Kilgore, S. (1982). *High school achievement: Public, Catholic and private schools compared.* New York: Basic Books.

Cox, D. R. (1970). *The analysis of binary data.* London: Methuen.

Cox, D. R. (1972). Regression models and life tables. *Journal of the Royal Statistical Society, B34*, 187-220.

Cox, D. R. (1975). Partial likelihood. *Biometrika, 62*, 269-276.

Cox, D. R., & Lewis, P. A. W. (1966). *The statistical analysis of events.* London: Chapman & Hall.

Cox, D. R., & Oakes, D. (1983). *The analysis of survival data.* New York: Chapman & Hall.

Diekman, A., & Mitter, P. (1983). The "sickle-hypothesis": A time-dependent Poisson model with applications to deviant behavior and occupational mobility. *Journal of Mathematical Sociology, 9*, 85-101.

Diekman, A., & Mitter, P. (1984). A comparison of the "sickle function" with alternative stochastic models of divorce rates. In A. Diekman & P. Mitter (Eds.), *Stochastic modeling of social processes* (pp. 123-153). Orlando, FL: Academic Press.

DiPrete, T. A. (1981). Unemployment over the life cycle: Racial differences and the effects of changing economic conditions. *American Journal of Sociology, 87*, 286-307.

Dixon, W. J. (Ed.). (1985). *BMDP statistical software manual.* Berkeley: University of California Press.

Duncan, G., & Morgan, J. N. (1985). The Panel Study of Income Dynamics. In G. L. Elder (Ed.), *Life course dynamics* (pp. 50-74). Ithaca, NY: Cornell University Press.

Duncan, O. D. (1984a). Measurement and structure: Strategies for the design and analysis of subjective survey data. In C. F. Turner & E. Martin (Eds.), *Surveying subjective phenomena* (Vol. 1, pp. 179-229). New York: Russell Sage Foundation.

Duncan, O. D. (1984b). Rasch measurement: Further examples and discussion. In C. F. Turner & E. Martin (Eds.), *Surveying subjective phenomena* (Vol. 2, pp. 367-403). New York: Russell Sage Foundation.

Duncan, O. D. (1985a). New light on the 16-fold table. *American Journal of Sociology, 91*, 88-128.

Duncan, O. D. (1985b). Some models of response uncertainty for panel analysis. *Social Science Research, 14*, 126-141.

Efron, B. (1977). The efficiency of Cox's likelihood function for censored data. *Journal of the American Statistical Association, 72*, 557-565.

Farewell, V. T., & Prentice, R. L. (1980). The approximation of partial likelihood with emphasis on case-control studies. *Biometrics, 67*, 273-278.

Featherman, D. L., & Hauser, R. M. (1978). *Opportunity and change.* New York: Academic Press.

Fergusson, D. M., Horwood, J. T., & Shannon, F. T. (1984). A proportional hazards model of family breakdown. *Journal of Marriage and the Family, 47*, 539-549.

Fienberg, S. (1980). *The analysis of cross-classified categorical data* (2nd ed.). Cambridge: MIT Press.

Flinn, C. J., & Heckman, J. J. (1982). New methods for analyzing individual event histories. In S. Leinhardt (Ed.), *Sociological methodology 1982* (pp. 99-140). San Francisco: Jossey-Bass.

Freeman, J., Carroll, G. L., & Hannan, M. T. (1983). The liability of newness: Age dependence in organizational death rates. *American Sociological Review, 48*, 692-710.

Glenn, N. D. (1977). *Cohort analysis.* Beverly Hills, CA: Sage.

Goodman, L. A. (1979). Simple models for the analysis of association in class-classifications having ordered categories. *Journal of the American Statistical Association, 76*, 320-334.

Grusky, D. B. (1983). Industrialization and the status attainment process: The thesis of industrialism reconsidered. *American Sociological Review, 48*, 494-506.

Haberman, S. J. (1977). Log-linear models and frequency tables with small expected cell counts. *Annals of Statistics, 5*, 1148-1169.

Haberman, S. J. (1978). *Analysis of qualitative data: Vol. 1. Introductory topics.* New York: Academic Press.

Heckman, J. J. (1981). Statistical models for discrete panel data. In C. F. Manski & D. McFadden (Eds.), *Structural analysis of discrete data with econometric applications* (pp. 114-178). Cambridge: MIT Press.

Heckman, J. J., & Borjas, G. (1980). Does unemployment cause future unemployment? Definitions, questions, and answers from a continuous model of heterogeneity and state dependence. *Econometrica, 47*, 247-283.

Heckman, J. J., & Honore, B. E. (1989). The identifiability of the competing risks model. *Biometrika, 76*, 525-530.

Heckman, J. J., & Singer, B. (1982). Population heterogeneity in demographic models. In K. C. Land & A. Rogers (Eds.), *Multidimensional mathematical demography* (pp. 567-598). New York: Academic Press.

Heckman, J. J., & Singer, B. (1984). A method for minimizing the impact of distributional assumptions in econometric models for duration data. *Econometrica, 52*, 271-320.

Heckman, J. J., & Walker, J. R. (1987). Using goodness of fit and other criteria to choose among competing duration models: A case of study of Hutterite data. In C. C. Clogg (Ed.), *Sociological methodology 1987* (pp. 247-307). Washington, DC: American Sociological Association.

Hogan, D. P. (1978). The variable order of events in the life course. *American Sociological Review, 43*, 573-586.

Hogan, D. P. (1981). *Transitions and social change: The early lives of American men.* New York: Academic Press.

Hogan, D. P., & Kertzer, D. I. (1986). Migration patterns during Italian urbanization: 1865-1921. *Demography, 22*, 309-352.

Hogan, D. P., & Kitagawa, E. M. (1985). The impact social status, family structure, and neighborhood on the fertility of black adolescents. *American Journal of Sociology, 90*, 825-855.

Holford, T. R. (1980). The analysis of rates and survivorship using log-linear models. *Biometrics, 65*, 159-165.

Hout, M. (1984). Status, autonomy, and training in occupational mobility. *American Journal of Sociology, 89*, 1379-1409.

Kalbfleisch, J. D., & Prentice, R. L. (1980). *The statistical analysis of failure time data.* New York: John Wiley.

Kandel, D. B., Shaffran, C., & Yamaguchi, K. (1985). *Life Event History Analysis Program* (PFSU Document No. 13). Unpublished manuscript, Columbia University, School of Public Health.

Kandel, D. B., & Yamaguchi, K. (1987). Job mobility and drug use: An event history analysis. *American Journal of Sociology, 92*, 836-878.

Koch, G. G., Johnson, E. D., & Tolly, H. D. (1972). A linear model approach to the analysis of survival and extent of disease in multidimensional contingency tables. *Journal of the American Statistical Association, 67*, 783-796.

Koike, K. (1983). Internal labor markets: Workers in large firms. In T. Shirai (Ed.), *Contemporary industrial relations in Japan* (pp. 29-62). Madison: University of Wisconsin Press.

Lachman, M. E. (1985). Personal efficacy in middle and old age: Differential and normative patterns of change. In G. L. Elder (Ed.), *Life course dynamics* (pp. 188-216). Ithaca, NY: Cornell University Press.

Laird, N., & Olivier, D. (1981). Covariance analysis of censored survival data using log-linear analysis techniques. *Journal of the American Statistical Association, 76*, 231-240.

LaRossa, R., & LaRossa, M. (1981). *Transition to parenthood: How infants change families.* Beverly Hills, CA: Sage.

Lawless, J. F. (1982). *Statistical models and methods for lifetime data.* New York: John Wiley.

Lehrer, E. (1984). The impact of child mortality on spacing by parity: A Cox-regression model. *Demography, 21*, 323-337.

Liang, K., & Zeger, S. L. (1986). Longitudinal data analysis using generalized linear models. *Biometrika, 73*, 13-22.

Liang, K., & Zeger, S. L. (1989). A class of logistic regression models for multivariate binary time series. *Journal of the American Statistical Association, 84*, 447-451.

Lillard, L. A., & Waite, L. J. (1990). *A joint model of childbearing and marital disruption.* Paper presented at the annual meeting of the American Sociological Association, Washington, DC.

Little, R. J. A., & Rubin, D. B. (1987). *Statistical analysis with missing data.* New York: John Wiley.

Liu, P. Y., & Crowley, J. (1978). *Large sample theory for the MLE based on Cox's regression model for survival data* (Technical Report No. 1, Biostatistics). Madison: University of Wisconsin, Wisconsin Clinical Career Center.

Mare, R. D., Winship, C., & Kubitschek, W. N. (1984). The transition from youth to adult: Understanding the age pattern of employment. *American Journal of Sociology, 90,* 326-358.

Marini, M. M. (1984a). Age and sequencing norms in the transition to adulthood. *Social Forces, 63,* 229-244.

Marini, M. M. (1984b). The order of events in the transition to adulthood. *Sociology of Education, 57,* 63-83.

Mason, W. M., & Fienberg, S. E. (Eds.). (1985). *Cohort analysis in social research.* New York: Springer-Verlag.

Massey, D. S. (1987). Understanding Mexican migration to the United States. *American Journal of Sociology, 92,* 1332-1403.

McCullagh, P., & Nelder, J. A. (1989). *Generalized linear models* (2nd ed.). New York: Chapman & Hill.

Michael, R. T., & Tuma, N. B. (1985). Entry into marriage and parenthood by young men and women. *Demography, 22,* 309-352.

Morgan, J. N., Dickinson, J., Dickinson, K., Benus, J., & Duncan, G. J. (1974). *Five thousand American families: Patterns of economic progress* (Vol. 1). Ann Arbor: Institute for Social Research.

Morgan, S. P., & Rindfuss, R. R. (1985). Marital disruption: Structural and temporal dimensions. *American Journal of Sociology, 90,* 1055-1077.

Namboodiri, K., & Suchindran, C. M. (1987). *Life table techniques and their applications.* New York: Academic Press.

Oakes, D. (1977). The asymptotic information in censored data. *Biometrika, 64,* 441-448.

Petersen, T. (1988). Analyzing change over time in a continuous dependent variable: Specification and estimation of continuous state space hazard rate models. In C. C. Clogg (Ed.), *Sociological methodology 1988* (pp. 137-164). Washington, DC: American Sociological Association.

Petersen, T. (1991). Time-aggregation bias in continuous time hazard rate models. In P. M. Marsden (Ed.), *Sociological methodology 1991.* Oxford: Basil Blackwell.

Prentice, R. L., & Farewell, V. T. (1984). Relative risk and odds ratio regression. *Annual Review of Public Health, 7,* 35-58.

Prentice, R. L., & Gloeckler, L. A. (1978). Regression analysis of grouped survival data with application to breast cancer. *Biometrics, 34,* 57-67.

Prentice, R. L., & Self, G. S. (1983). Asymptotic distribution theory for Cox-type regression models with general relative risk form. *Annals of Statistics, 11,* 804-813.

Preston, D. L., & Clarkson, D. B. (1983). SURVREG: A program for the interactive analysis of survival regression models. *American Statistician, 37,* 174.

Raftery, A. E. (1986). Choosing models for cross-classifications. *American Journal of Sociology, 51,* 145-146.

Rao, C. R. (1973). *Linear statistical inference and its applications* (2nd ed.). New York: John Wiley.

Riley, M. W., Johnson, M. E., & Fones A. (Eds.). (1972). *Aging and society: A sociology of age stratification* (Vol. 3). New York: Russell Sage Foundation.

Rossi, A. (1968). Transition to parenthood. *Journal of Marriage and the Family, 30,* 26-39.

Sakamoto, Y., Ishiguro, M., & Kitagawa, G. (1986). *Akaike information criterion statistics.* Boston: D. Reidel.

Schluchter, M. D., & Jackson, K. L. (1989). Log-linear analysis of censored survival data with partially observed covariates. *Journal of the American Statistical Association, 84,* 42-52.

Schwarz, G. (1978). Estimating the dimension of a model. *Annals of Statistics, 6,* 461-464.

Sørensen, A., & Tuma, N. B. (1981). Labor market structures and job mobility. In D. Treiman & R. V. Robinson (Eds.), *Research in social stratification and mobility* (Vol. 1, pp. 67-94). New York: Academic Press.

Sumiya, M. (1974a). Nihonkeki roshi kankeiron no saikentou: I. Nenkousei no kokusai hikaku [Japanese labor-management relations reviewed: Part I. An international comparison of seniority-wage system]. *Nihon Rodo Kyokai Zasshi* [Journal of the Japanese Labor Association], *194.*

Sumiya, M. (1974b). Nihonkeki roshi kankeiron no saikentou: II. Nenkousei no ronri o megutte [Japanese labor-management relations reviewed: Part II. A discussion on the *nenko* system]. *Nihon Rodo Kyokai Zasshi* [Journal of the Japanese Labor Association], *194.*

Taira, K. (1962). Characteristics of Japanese labor markets. *Economic Development and Cultural Change, 10,* 150-168.

Teachman, J. D. (1982). Methodological issues in the analysis of family formation and dissolution. *Journal of Marriage and the Family, 44,* 1037-1053.

Teachman, J. D., & Heckert, D. A. (1985). The declining significance of first-birth timing. *Demography, 22,* 185-198.

Teachman, J. D., & Schollaert, P. T. (1989). Gender of children and birth timing. *Demography, 26,* 411-423.

Tominaga, K. (1979). *Nohon no kaiso kouzou* [The structure of stratification in Japan]. Tokyo: University of Tokyo Press.

Trussell, J., & Richards, T. (1985). Correcting unmeasured heterogeneity in hazard models using the Heckman-Singer procedure. In N. B. Tuma (Ed.), *Sociological methodology 1985* (pp. 242-276). San Francisco: Jossey-Bass.

Tsiatis, A. A. (1981). A large sample study of Cox's regression model. *Annals of Statistics, 9,* 93-108.

Tuma, N. B. (1976). Rewards, resources and the rate of mobility: A nonstationary multivariate stochastic model. *American Sociological Review, 41,* 338-360.

Tuma, N. B. (1979). *Invoking RATE.* Unpublished program manual.

Tuma, N. B. (1985). Effects of labor market structure on job-shift patterns. In J. J. Heckman & B. Singer (Eds.), *Longitudinal analysis of labor market data* (pp. 327-365). Cambridge: Cambridge University Press. (Original work published 1978)

Tuma, N. B., & Hannan, M. T. (1979). Approaches to the censoring problem in analysis of event histories. In K. F. Schuessler (Ed.), *Sociological methodology 1979* (pp. 209-240). San Francisco: Jossey-Bass.

Tuma, N. B., & Hannan, M. T. (1984). *Social dynamics.* New York: Academic Press.

Wong, W. H. (1986). Theory of partial likelihood. *Annals of Statistics, 14,* 88-123.

Wu, L. L. (1989). Issues in smoothing empirical hazard rates. In C. C. Clogg (Ed.), *Sociological methodology 1989* (pp. 127-159). Oxford: Basil Blackwell.

Wu, L. L., & Tuma, N. B. (1990). Local hazard models. In C. C. Clogg (Ed.), *Sociological methodology 1990* (pp. 141-180). Oxford: Basil Blackwell.

Yamaguchi, K. (1986). Alternative approaches to unobserved heterogeneity in the analysis of repeatable events. In N. B. Tuma (Ed.), *Sociological methodology 1986* (pp. 213-249). Washington, DC: American Sociological Association.

Yamaguchi, K. (1987a). Event-history analysis: Its contribution to modeling and causal inference. *Sociological Theory and Methods, 2*, 61-82.

Yamaguchi, K. (1987b). Models for comparing mobility tables. *American Sociological Review, 52*, 482-494.

Yamaguchi, K. (1990a). *Accelerated failure time regression model with a regression model of surviving fraction: An application to the analysis of permanent employment in Japan* (UCLA Statistics Series 57). Los Angeles: University of California.

Yamaguchi, K. (1990b). Logit and multinomial logit models for discrete-time event-history analysis: A causal analysis of interdependent discrete-state processes. *Quality and Quantity, 24*, 323-341.

Yamaguchi, K., & Kandel, D. B. (1985a). Dynamic relationship between premarital cohabitation and illicit drug use: An event history analysis of role selection and role socialization. *American Sociological Review, 50*, 530-546.

Yamaguchi, K., & Kandel, D. B. (1985b). On the resolution of role incompatibility: A life event history analysis of family roles and marijuana use. *American Journal of Sociology, 90*, 1284-1325.

Yamaguchi, K., & Kandel, D. B. (1987). Drug use and other determinants of premarital pregnancy and its outcome: A dynamic analysis of competing life events. *Journal of Marriage and the Family, 49*, 257-270.

Yi, K. M., Walker, J., & Honore, A. B. (1986). *CTM: A user's guide.* Unpublished manuscript, University of Chicago, National Opinion Research Center.

About the Author

Kazuo Yamaguchi is Professor of Sociology at the University of Chicago; he was previously affiliated with the University of California, Los Angeles, where the manuscript was prepared. He received his undergraduate education at the University of Tokyo, Japan, and his graduate degrees from the University of Chicago. He taught at Columbia University and UCLA prior to joining the faculty at the University of Chicago. His articles on methodology, social mobility, demography, the life course, and drug use have appeared in major journals, including *American Sociological Review, American Journal of Sociology, Sociological Methodology, Journal of the American Statistical Association, Quality and Quantity, Demography, Journal of Marriage and the Family,* and *American Journal of Public Health.* In addition to event history analysis, his methodological specialties include categorical data analysis based on log-linear and log-bilinear models. More than two thirds of his published articles are about one of these methods or their substantive applications.